I0429005

The
Teatarian

A belief in economic and social freedom

T.L Crain

DEDICATION

I guess the initial dedication should be to the infernal force that compels me to write – that keeps me awake at night. This book wouldn't have been possible had it not been for my best friend, Stephen, who has inspired me by allowing me to see most of this great country. He is the force that nudges me when I want to give up on the country. I am forever grateful for his presence.

Table of Contents

Author Quotes

We have become slaves to the system only because we allow it to happen.

Who deserves the most blame, the temptress or the tempted?
Blame falls fully on the shoulders of the one with whom the public has placed their trust.

We sometimes become so involved in our party or candidate winning that we forget about liberty.

We must always do what's right in our hearts unless it violates the rights of others.

An education is simply the foundation on which to learn.

Everything we do today is a step toward who we will be tomorrow.

Paths are for the apathetic. The curious will always blaze a new trail. It's the curious who invents, discovers, and creates.

Clouding issues is no longer a past-time, but has become a way of life for most politicians and their flock.

All the wealthy politicians sit in their towers of ivory and preach to us about economic & social justice.

Totalitarianism has always been done in the name of the greater good. Those who oppose are said to hate the poor.

No matter the school from which we graduate, a life of home schooling begins.

Necessity is the mother of invention. Government regulation is an invention's worst enemy.

Progressives love to talk about sustainability, yet their economic policies aren't sustainable.

Progressives believe crony capitalism is okay as long as it furthers their cause. <u>Anything for the cause,</u> because they believe it just.

Those who place all their trust in government, no matter the party in charge, is destined for disappointment.

We are all unique individuals and should take pride in the fact that no one on the planet can be just like us. When we reach the end, and we have lived that life to the fullest without expense to others, we can go with a smile.

Capitalists spread wealth through job creation. Socialist spread wealth through slothfulness. Which most benefits society?

Too many people falsely believe a free USA will last forever. They forget freedom isn't guaranteed – it's earned.

Capitalism is poverty by choice or chance. Socialism is poverty by force.

What is a Teatarian?

As the tagline says in the seal, it's where the Tea Party meets libertarianism. In its beginning the Tea Party movement was only about smaller government, fiscal responsibility, and embracing the free market. Some of the Tea Party groups had a strict policy against discussing social issues. There is at least one that somewhat still applies those rules, albeit loosely. In time libertarians have been slowly forced out of these groups. It's for this reason the Tea Party Movement has taken on the image of a conservative organization.

Another problem with the Tea Party is that it seems some are in it only for the money. Your first thought might be to say that the IRS must have had reason to target Tea Party groups. It seems some of the Tea Party Groups that will say anything for money haven't applied for a 501(c), at least to my knowledge.

Many of the Constitutionalists and libertarian minded people have begun distancing themselves from the – now social conservative – Tea Party. This, in part, is why I began the search for a new name for my blog, Tea Party Tempest. My blog originally began as I've Got a Bitch. Because that name had always been, let's say, a bit too descriptive, I had pondered other names. Once I became associated with the Tea Party I decided a new name must show that connection.

I Still believe in the original beliefs of the Tea Party movement, and for that reason I didn't want to completely disassociate myself from the name. By combining TEA(Taxed Enough Already) and libertarian I came up with Teatarian. I could only laugh when I later learned it was often used as a derogatory term by those who hold disdain for both the Tea Party and libertarians. I find it ironic that that whose who we have been labeled "liberal" are far less liberal than libertarians.

It is for those liberal views on social issues that libertarians often find themselves at odds with the current Tea Party Conservative.

Over the years I've written thousands of words that I believe shows my consistency with the Teatarian view. I confess to having at times defended Republicans when I shouldn't. Sometimes we find ourselves caught up in the battle to defend our choice of a candidate over another. I'm sure at times I've attempted to explain away mistakes made by politicians. I will also confess that there have been times when I believed a politician when I shouldn't. Even I can sometimes be sold a bill of goods.

I also believe a Teatarian should be observant in human behavior, even our own. I learned from Edward Bernays that politics is often simply manipulating the human mind. Bernays said it was better to convince people of a need for a product rather than the product brand itself. Instead of advertising a certain brand of cigarettes Bernays decided to expand the market and used the women's suffrage movement to make smoking popular among women. Bernays didn't invent modern marketing techniques, but he surely took it to new levels. It is for this reason he is considered the father of propaganda. A good Teatarian will always be on the lookout for political movements that are no more that marketing campaigns.

This books contains a selection of fully edited and sometimes updated blog post I made over the years. It also contains unseen segments from a book I ultimately decided not to release. A look into the past will show the Teatarian view should be one of consistency.

Ideology

A World of Followers

Published on
3/14/14 1:42 AM

I think I finally understand the world around me – or at least why it is traveling in its current direction. It was a simple post on Facebook that made me become aware of the entire picture. The graphic apparently circulated enough that Snopes saw fit to add it to its long list of internet myths. When it came to my attention I was shocked that any single individual could believe that Facebook legal staff could pass laws.

The graphic indicated that Facebook passed a law to ban all talk of religion. It was presented as a continuation to the war on Christians.

Each day there is something new about which people become outraged. Some of it is fact, some a blend of fact and fiction, and some obvious mistruths. We have Alex Jones who has a huge following. There are those who accept everything he says as gospel. There are the Art Bell followers who do the same. I'm not here to say what is and what isn't truth from either of those. All that interest me, is why do others believe almost 100%.

People love a conspiracy. People love a good mystery novel. I'm sure science can point to an area of the brain that is stimulated by such things. But I think there is more to it than simple mind stimulation. There are the people who are skeptical of everything – to a fault. There are those who often look at events with cold logic.

For now, let's stick to those who want to believe and how they are being manipulated. There are items like the fake graphic about Facebook banning religion. Someone likely did

3

that for amusement. Many love to watch the gullible fall for the obviously outrageous.

There are those who do the same thing for power and money. Marketing is this type of manipulation. Someone made a fortune selling Pet Rocks. Consumers didn't buy them because they were anything more than a rock, but because they made it become a novelty – something popular. They bought the name and packaging.

Each day people are sucked into these Nigerian money scams. People open virus filled files because they promise riches. This is because people have a deep seeded need to believe. People need to believe government will keep them safe or that there really is a pot of gold at the end of the rainbow.

Just this week there was a local incident where a York, SC police officer shot and severely injured a 70 year old man simply because he exited the car with his walking cane. We are seeing these incidents happening daily all over the country. That in itself is a problem, but possibly the bigger problem are those who make excuses for the officers. There are those who say, "The old man should have followed the rules." We now live in a society where it has become acceptable for government to kill innocent people simply because they broke the rules.

We have the NSA, politicians, and citizens alike who support spying on innocent Americans. We have the CIA killing people with drones, occasionally Americans. Many support these actions. Too many people want to believe what they see and hear, especially on the internet and television. It doesn't matter if your political orientation is left, right, or middle, you are likely victim of falling for propaganda and mistruths. We find people along the full IQ spectrum who are acceptable to propaganda.

The human has some innate need to believe. This is especially true if the information comes from friends or those in the media and government they trust. Those people are often themselves influenced by propaganda and mistruths. Many people don't intentionally lie except in cases of scams and practical jokes, or to cover their butt.

The only thing we can do is to take no information for granted. Unless we become a society of moderate skeptics then we will fall for many evils. The people of Nazi Germany put their faith in government. Governments, monarchies, and oligarchies throughout history have committed atrocities against their citizens.

Become aware of your surroundings. When in the grocery store know who is behind you. When your best friend tells you something – double check. When your favorite politician or television/radio personality tells you something, double check the information. Our generation has been blessed with the greatest research tool ever devised by mankind. We have the knowledge of Einstein at our fingertips – we must take advantage of those tools.

When you see someone with the title doctor or nuclear engineer, don't assume they know their job. More people in our society are addicted to prescription drugs than those made illegal by government. People pop those pills into their mouths simply because a doctor tells them they should.

Justina Pelletier was taken from her parents because one doctor disagreed with another. The parents were treated like criminals simply because they sought the best medical treatment for their daughter. This young girl is now near death because her parents were not allowed to seek the best medical treatment.

Ladies, gentlemen, and the gullible, I present to you your government and the police state that you have allowed them to create. We now live in a society where the lower middle class will be fined because they can't afford health insurance. We live in a society where police attacked and broke the bones of a 90 year old, or shot a 70 year old for the simple act of getting out of his car with a cane. We live in a society where Stop and

Frisk is an accepted practice. Our world is one where we allow government employees to frisk our bodies before boarding a plane. We willingly step into machines that will electronically remove our clothing.

We buy goods and services we don't need simply because of what we are told. We lock ourselves in endless cellphone contracts simply because we must have the latest phone. We go into debt for houses and cars we can't afford. We demand government keep us safe at any cost. We never want our comfortable lives to end. For these things you have gladly traded your liberty. You are willing to vote for someone who simply offered *Change* when they had no history to back up their words.

I will still cry for you when it is your child the government takes and nearly kills. I will cry when it is your mother or father that is killed on a lonely highway by an overzealous representative of the police state. I won't cry when you lose your home and car you never could afford. I won't cry when your child ends up in the hospital almost dead because of prescription medicines, or when the government refuses your heart operation – because it is your fault.

The Following

Published on
3/16/14 4:05 AM

There is a television show titled *The Following*. The story begins when a college literature professor becomes enraptured by the works of Edgar Allan Poe. He teaches these many writings with such passion students become as enthralled as their professor. In time they become so consumed by their passion that they explore the dark world of murder. For these people it is not cold and ruthless, but emotional and calculated.

In time those students grow into adults and become a part of everyday society. They are doctors, lawyers, police, and FBI agents. No matter their current lives they have this attachment to their old professor, Joe Carroll. They do his bidding without hesitation. These former students will gladly die for their leader. This former professor, simply because he had a passion for an author, unwittingly created a cult.

We often think of cults as David Koresh and the Branch Davidians where he and many members died in an assault by the ATF. There was Jim Jones and the Peoples Temple where they drank poison in mass suicide. The Manson Family might be the most infamous of them all because of their horrendous murder of actress Sharon Tate.

There are many other cults that exist in the world today. Some say Scientology is a cult, and some even apply that label to the Mormon church. But we must ask—what is a cult? We typically think of a cult as a group built around an individual and a set of beliefs. Often the center of a cult is religious in nature.

Below is one meaning.

Cult:

Sociology . a group having a sacred ideology and a set of rites centering around their sacred symbols.

This brings me to another question. Can a political party become a cult? I say most definitely. There are those who follow their favorite political party or figurehead with with great fervor. Some have likened Ron Paul followers to a cult. I can only say that a few followers act cult-like.

I'd define the political cult follower as one who defends their party or ideological stance even when it shifts to a position they previously argued against – simply because the leaders tell them they should. They will throw logic and facts out the window to defend their position. I once used a sports analogy on how it's all about pulling for your favorite team, which still applies. But I have to sometimes wonder if it runs much deeper.

As I wrote in *A World of Followers* after watching the video of a police officer gun down an unarmed 70 year old man, people still supported the officer's actions. There is no part of my mind that can believe the officer didn't act in haste. This happens because people have been taught to trust the police. This elderly man wound up in the hospital simply because he trusted the officer. He might have been dead had it not been for the officer's wild, uncontrolled shooting. The wife of the elderly man is lucky she wasn't wounded in the uncontrolled gunfire.

I once heard a democratic operative say that for generations his family has always voted Democratic. This means the man's ancestry voted for the people who installed Jim Crow laws. They voted for the people that forbade blacks to eat in white establishments. His family voted for the likes of George Wallace. This same democrat will hail the party's stand in the Civil Rights movement.

The Republican Party will do the same thing. There are those who have proclaimed loyalty to the party for generations. Those same people who talk today about secession or smaller government hail Abraham Lincoln as the great savior – the man who burned much of the south and declared secession illegal. This is the same man that through his Emancipation Proclamation freed only the slaves in the Confederate States of America and those who supported them – not those in the North. He is the man that suspended habius corpus and arrested war protestors.

No party is fully innocent. Even the founders should never be put on this untouchable pedestal because they as well made many mistakes, one is allowing slavery in the beginning. Few people want to look at history honestly. History shows us there is nothing pure and innocent about any nation or political party. If we want to build a better world we must at least look at the past with open eyes.

The Teatarian

To create this better world we have to stop defending bad politicians and political parties that have only one agenda, power and money. Many Republicans excused Bush, while many Democrats do the same with Obama, while both men do many of the same things. These men have one thing in common, both grew government at a rate not seen since FDR.

Our political parties have become cult-like. Ronald Reagan was a prime example. Although he did do some good things, he increased government. I can list many things, but that can come another time. What's important now is there has been a cult built around him. There are people who become extremely angry if you say anything negative about the former president, or they will make excuses for his actions.

President Obama had a cult following that was astounding. This was a man who could do no wrong. He was given the Nobel Peace Prize before doing anything notable. His following came simply because people were fed up with typical politics and he promised change. We were a country that had war fatigue – he promised peace. After five years we all know that it was only empty promises. His cult is slowly falling apart. To maintain a cult you must occasionally provide a miracle or simply awe the following. The other way to maintain the following is to die and let mythology fill in the miracle blanks.

Everyone keeps hoping the country will change, but they are unwilling to participate in that change. The system has been rigged. The two parties have colluded to make the system insure those two, not only survive, but dominate the political scene. They have created their oligarchy that feeds the crony system. Corporations are blamed for being too powerful and buying political favors. Only the corrupt can be bought.

Both parties have their cult-like following. The following spends countless hours spreading party propaganda. If you keep supporting the cult nothing will change. The only way to save the country is to get rid of the cults. Get people together who think like you. Find a candidate you like, but not one that is a member of the cult. Once you do that, write that name onto the ballot. Once enough of these people are elected, they can change the laws that support the two cult system. Doing the same thing over and over with the same results is the true definition of insanity.

If you have a family member that cannot break from the cult, take them to a detox center. Stop being a follower. Let's actually change the system. Sure we can set term limits, but that won't stop the cults from controlling the game. As a participant of the Tea Party I thought like many others that we could take over the GOP. I know now that won't happen. The cult will not let outsiders change the game. In that case there is only one option – end the game – shut down the political cults. Just be careful that in the end you don't simply create new cults. If it proves impossible to prevent new cults, we must at last have many more than the current two party oligarchy.

Conservatives vs libertarians: The Divided Tea Party

Published on
11/4/13 2:21 PM

I was reading the college thesis of Washington Times reporter, Jessica Chasmar and she reminded me of the day I stood on the Capitol lawn on 9/12, 2009. That day I saw a movement that I believed could change the country forever. That was one of the proudest moments of my life. I had finally become a part of something great.

Today, late 2013, the progressives have full control of government. We see far left policies as norm of the day. We are witnessing one of the greatest government takeovers (Affordable Care Act) go into effect with disastrous results so far.

What happened to the Tea Party? It's being torn apart by those who use its name for money or power. It's being torn apart by those that believe it is a conservative movement. If you are not a social conservative you are often ostracized by the movement.

The Tea Party was originally the accretion of people who came together because of TARP and other fiscal matters. For once the social agenda had taken a backseat and the Tea Party managed to make significant change in the 2010 House.

Today the Tea Party is unpopular and often viewed as racist, or filled with bigots. There are instances of both, while I still believe there is a silent majority that are not either of those things. There are Tea Party websites that allow comments that can only feed negative views of the movement. It's time we stand up to those segments that put the Tea Party in a bad light.

Because of the weakening Tea Party movement we now have a progressive government and it's moving more left as we speak. Unless social conservatives can form a truce with libertarian minded members then the country for which we had hoped will never be. We will find ourselves back in the 30's and FDR.

The Democratic Party knows that in any debate or election against a social conservative all he/she has to do is bring up social issues. The social conservative candidate will try to dance around the topic, but will in the end call for bigger government by demanding it maintain it's hold on marriage and the uneven application of taxes. One justice stated there were 1100 statues that separate married from unmarried couples or single individuals.

Social conservatives and libertarians must find common ground or the country is lost. I believe that common ground must always be less government. Obama once said we must all sacrifice. We know he meant that only others sacrifice and that government should grow. In order to make government sacrifice we must first sacrifice ourselves. We must give up some of our favorite government protections. We must trust in the individual – ourselves – and the free market. Until the day most Americans can think of all citizens as equal and demand they all be treated equally under the law, the progressives are winning. If all are equal under the law then the progressives will no longer have the need for laws that support various citizen sub groups.

We cannot favor tax subsidies for housing. Through mortgage subsidies the government is buying the average American's vote. In time, without tax subsidies, the mortgage rates would come in line with the natural free market. Are you willing to sacrifice for the future?

Home subsidies are only an example. It doesn't matter if it's government sanctioned marriage or subsidized infrastructure, we must be willing to sacrifice for the future. If libertarians and social conservatives stand divided the $17 trillion debt will be nothing compared to future debt. Many Americans have become too comfortable and secure. Many believe the USA will always be the strongest nation on the planet. We saw during the great depression what a progressive government can do to a powerful nation. It was put on its knees to the point that Japan thought they could conquer the once great giant. It was only the war with Japan that saved the country from progressive rule.

It's not too late. Conservatives, go to your libertarian counterparts and think how much you are alike and not dwell on the differences. At least for today leave the social battles on the local level and work to free the federal government from progressives.

Stop the name calling and reach out to progressives and explain how smaller government can work. Teach them to trust in state rule and not federal rule. Teach them history and how power corrupts absolutely. Make sure you are always the calm voice in the room. Some think there can never be a Hitler or Stalin in the USA, but in some ways we already have them. We have elected presidents that are picked from a small list of party approved people. We have presidents who through executive order can create law. Yes America, we are already living under tyranny in open disguise. United we stand, divided we fall. It's time to Unite America. To do that we must first unite the Tea Party. Become a Teatarian today.

Remember, libertarian isn't a party, it's a belief in individualism.

Are you an Interventionist or a Non-Interventionist?

Published on
10/26/13 9:50 AM

Some days a light goes off and you begin to see things in a different way. Today is one of those days. For too long we have argued over who was what politically. The Democrats say they are doing what's best for the country, while Republicans and libertarians say the same. Sometimes we get so wrapped up in party we forget to think. There is a simple solution.

We are all interventionist or non-interventionist. It doesn't matter if it's social politics or foreign events, the terms can be applied. Can it be this cut and dry? Can we be an interventionist on something and a non-interventionist on others? Remember the age old adage "Mind your own business." Our ancestors have passed those wise words along through the ages. The non-interventionist is simply the same thing.

The interventionist often uses the power of government to do their bidding. They don't want other people to eat certain foods so they elect people who are also interventionist.

Interventionist believe most people aren't capable of self governance. There are some people who are, and will always be, dependent on others. Even a non-interventionist believes in helping those who ask for help. The interventionist doesn't wait for them to ask for help, but forces help on those in need as well as those who aren't.

Some of us have been looking for a way to bring like minded people together, but find that difficult because of labels and misguided perceptions. I find that I agree with Democrats on many things. We even occasionally agree on the best solution. It's because of labels that we cannot find enough common ground on which to work effectively, even though all political persuasions agree that government is broke.

In the end it comes down to those who want more government and those who want less. There are those who believe government is more efficient than private industry, while others see the opposite. No matter if it's government or private interest, I think most can agree we don't want them in our lives. We don't want government or business intervening in our lives. Because we can agree on this, we find that Democrat, Republican, and libertarian can be non-interventionists.

lib·er·al
1. open to new behavior or opinions and willing to discard traditional values.
"they have more liberal views toward marriage and divorce than some people"(of education) concerned 2. mainly with broadening a person's general knowledge and experience, rather than with technical or professional training.

con·serv·a·tive
1. holding to traditional attitudes and values and cautious about change or innovation, typically in relation to politics or religion.

2. a person who is averse to change and holds to traditional values and attitudes, typically in relation to politics.

re·pub·li·can
1. (of a form of government, constitution, etc.) belonging to, or characteristic of a republic.
advocating or supporting republican government.
"the republican movement"
2. a person advocating or supporting republican government.

lib·er·tar·i·an
1. an adherent of libertarianism.
"libertarian philosophy"
a person who advocates civil liberty.
2. Philosophy: a person who believes in the doctrine of free will.

pro·gres·sive
1. happening or developing gradually or in stages; proceeding step by step.
"a progressive decline in popularity"
2. (of a group, person, or idea) favoring or implementing social reform or new, liberal ideas.
"a relatively progressive governor"
3. a person advocating or implementing social reform or new, liberal ideas.
synonyms: innovator, reformer, reformist, liberal, libertarian More

Above are all the defined political terms. At first look we might say they point out the differences, but I see many similarities. For example, no one wants the country to not grow. Everyone wants it to move forward. I remember learning about the founders and how the liberals were for building a republic and wanting a free populous. Look at John Locke who founded liberalism, yet today there is a conservative leaning foundation named for him.

Labels and their meanings have changed over the decades.

Those with socialist and communist beliefs have hijacked some of the labels and parties. That's why we might be simplifying things by simply looking at everything in two ways, interventionist or non-interventionist. Which are you?

Dog and Pony Show Revisited (DAPS)

Published on
12/4/13 1:17 PM

I have written before about the dog and pony show that plays out before us each day. If the problem of the day is Obamacare, the media and the democrats will talk about immigration. Each problem is huge and blown out of proportion. Once again we were faced with shutdown of government and once again it was going to be a huge disaster. In the latest one I had driven 4,000 miles to see the Grand Canyon and wasn't sure I would be allowed in. (They did open it three days before I arrived.)

Each time they want the debt limit raised we are told the government will default on our debt if they don't get their way. While a few political and economic junkies know this is a lie, the rest of the country isn't sure. Most of the country has become numbed by the constant flow of lies. A few cling to the lies of their favorite party and happily pass them along to anyone who will listen. Too many, either out of ignorance or just happy to tow the party line, are willing participants in the dog and pony show.

Today one of the top stories is about an 11 year old girl that was selling mistletoe in Portland's, Oregon park. Yes, it is a heart warming story about the entrepreneurial spirit of a young American. The story is used to imply the young girl was treated harshly or unfairly. It is made to look like the entrepreneurial spirit is bad and begging is okay. Park officials stated correctly, begging is free speech, which has been upheld by the courts. New York has tried to ban panhandling in the past and has been successful in only limiting aggressive begging, or for reasons of safety.

The little girl has learned a valuable lesson. If park officials had given in, the girl would not have learned there are regulations that control street vending. She is learning a lesson in how to fight regulations and making them more sensible.

The lesson I truly hope she learns is to not become a part of the dog and pony show. She is being used to push a political agenda. I'm not saying the agenda is a bad one. I'm speaking solely to the game being played in her name. Things have worked out well for the young girl and she has had a wonderful learning experience.

Each day as we surf the daily news, or watch our favorite channels on television, we must remember that media has one purpose only, and that's to make money. Each story is calculated as to who will be drawn to their advertisers. This doesn't tell us if the information is right or wrong, it's just a reminder that it's all part of the dog and pony show. The news makes an effort to appear in the middle, but often appearances are deceiving. The middle is relative to the viewer's beliefs.

Today we all get a lot of our information from bloggers who don't have profits in mind. Some are part of the propaganda machine that drives candidate popularity. Many are people that have willingly become a part of their favorite dog and pony show. Then there are those who enjoy research and look for only truth. Sometimes the truth is hidden by the dog and pony show, but with enough perseverance it's out there.

We know the biggest dog and pony show of our era is climate change/global warming. There are some brilliant minds that participate in the show. They do so for a variety of reasons, some for research grants, or some just because it's the cool thing to do. Scientific participation in the dog and pony show can be dangerous. Millions could end up starving or it could cause economic collapse. The two major political parties are guilty of using the topic of climate change to their advantage. The dog and pony show is often filled with extremes on either side of the argument.

We must always look past the dogs and ponies if we are to advance this society in a civil manner. The dog and pony show has not only divided America, it has divided the world. We can't be fooled by those who sell tickets to the dog and pony show and then sit back and laugh. We must stop playing the party games and always think first about liberty and equality under the law. Some will always place their prejudices and bigotries first. That forces the rest of us to work harder to break down political lines. We must be wary of the two main political parties because they are major producers of dog and pony shows.

In 2008 the Democratic party had total control of government. They could have rushed through any legislation of their desire. Why didn't they legalize marijuana? Why didn't they pass the Dream Act, gay marriage, or immigration reform? The democrats had their entire agenda before them. They could have put many issues behind them. The reason they didn't is because they would have lost some of their best dog and pony shows. They would have lost issues on which to pledge promises come election time. The only major bill that passed was the Affordable Care Act. This is the only one that mattered because it grew government and gave them massive control. All the other issues are just shiny objects that are dangled before voters come election time.

Republicans are just as guilty. When they had complete power they fulfilled few promises. In every case where the Republican party had control, they increased spending (94 might be an exception) and grew government. That would have been the opportunity to dramatically reduce government by taking power back from the Executive Branch. They didn't because they love power and control as much as the democrats.

We have two ideological beliefs in this country. One segment believes in the most liberty possible and equality under the law. The other wants to control aspects of our lives, from the food we eat to the lives we live. Not all of either segment is in a single political party. Once we become entrapped by the dog and pony show we often become attached to a single political party. We must close our eyes to the show and think liberty.

The Perils of Laws and Perceptions

Published on
9/22/13 9:44 AM

I wrote this in response to an article about new tobacco taxes and the reasons for them. A respondent stated there were no conspiracies behind most things done by government. It has often been said that money is the root of all evil – coupled with the desire for power and you have the answer to most of the world's problems.

You are right, there are no conspiracies. If we follow the money we always find the force behind many of the things you mentioned(drug and alcohol laws). Statistics are padded and ignored to bring about the desired results. A statistician will tell you he or she can support any belief. Even when we ourselves look at raw numbers we can't be sure of the truth. I have looked deeply into DUI statistics. They will tell us how many people are killed each year in alcohol related accidents, or how many people are killed by drunk drivers.

What the statistics and proponents of laws don't tell us is that a DUI related accident doesn't mean the drinker was the cause of the accident. They don't tell us that speeding or reckless driving was the cause. We aren't told the road was covered in ice and it was truly just an accident. When a beer can is found on the roadside, or a weeks old empty in the floorboard, the accident becomes alcohol related. If the attending officer can smell what he/she believes to be alcohol, even if it's cough medicine, it becomes an alcohol related accident.

This is worth repeating again – we know speeding kills more people than other causes for traffic deaths. If DUI laws were really about saving lives, all speed limits would be lowered to 40 MPH. But then we have to look at speeding statistics themselves. Too often we see a 35 MPH zone on a section of road that was built for 50 MPH. People inevitably speed and police closely monitor these sections. This is done purely for revenue enhancement.

Government conditions people to believe propaganda. They begin ad campaigns telling us how evil drugs are and that the drunk driver is the biggest menace in the country. Yes, these things can be bad. Moderation is the solution to many of today's problems. Each week there seems to be the new big bad. Each week we lose more control over our lives.

We know terrorism exists around the world. The government wants us to believe the reason we have so little of it in this country is because of their fantastic work and NSA spying. I think the reasons are much lower for a different reason. Terrorist might come to this country with the intent of causing harm, but they discover what appears to be paradise for them. The point is, when government and the media is hyping something, we must listen with caution and an open mind.

Today's media doesn't come to their positions by force, it is purely agenda driven. It is a field which draws the progressive personality. Media owners want their businesses to be seen as reporting objectively. It's for this reason they choose a position they perceive to be the middle. Perception is relative to the viewer. Today the media drives perception and can easily distort the middle position.

The media loves dead bodies littering the streets and it's for that reason they cling to traffic accident scenes captioned by 'Drunk Driver.' Because they love death scenes the public can get a distorted view.

The same can be said for terrorism. When there is an act of terrorism the media will quickly avoid making the connection. It is only when no other official cause can be found will they come to the factual conclusion. This isn't because the media wants to hide acts of terror, but to maintain their perceived position of the middle. Because most acts of terrorist are by those of the Muslim faith – they hesitate. Some think this is because they believe the media is protecting the religion. It's because they worry more about maintaining their middle position than the facts of the story.

No matter if it's drugs, alcohol, or terrorism there is always the manipulation of perception. We are all guilty of trying to manipulate facts and statistics to support our point of view. These manipulations are done for many reasons, and sometimes done for what is believed to be the greater good. Who would complain about getting drunk drivers off the road? Who would complain about getting drug dealers off the streets? Most won't and the government knows this.

While some evils are magnified, others are glossed over. The reasons are often simple, there is no money in ending some evils. In an effort to make sure all Americans are equal under the law, we must also make sure all laws are equal to the truth.

I should note that this theory applies only to laws and statistics. When it comes to politics there are so many more variables. I was just reminded how the media was solidly behind the unknown Obama. There were obvious facts the media chose to ignore about the future president. That's an article unto itself. The Obama Syndrome speaks to that aspect

T. L. Crain

The lowercase libertarian

Published on
9/13/13 9:41 AM

In today's political environment more and more people are identifying with libertarianism. This often confuses some when they look at the Libertarian party and it's members. To some extent the Libertarian Party has been hijacked by anarchists and communists. It would take an article unto itself to fully explain how communists find their way into the Libertarian Party. True communists believe they can create a libertarian styled society and replace government with some board of elders. They fail to see that the board of elders is simply government under a different name.

When we hear the term libertarian tossed around we must pause and look to see if they are a true libertarian. Capital 'L' libertarians are those who belong to the party and can have varying political beliefs. The lowercase 'l' are those like myself who believe in all cases limited government is the best road to travel. We don't want the elimination of government or a major change in how government operates. We simply want less government and the right to self govern whenever possible.

I believe the founders intended for society to operate on the edge of anarchy, but far enough from the line of chaos that it doesn't become only the strongest survive. Any society needs rules by which people must live, but there must be limits placed on those rules and rulers. We too often elect someone to power and then turn our backs as they pass regulation after regulation. We are then shocked when we receive a parking ticket for parking in our own driveway because of an ordinance that prevents anyone from parking within thirty feet of the road. You might think this sounds ridiculous, but it actually happened in a Pittsburgh neighborhood.

The Teatarian

In my own little burg people woke in surprise after a three year battle to find they could only dispose trash in special yellow bags that can be purchased from only the county. Once citizens woke up and became aware they managed to get the silly law stricken from the books.

These are just two examples of thousands or millions of these things happening all over the country. These things can only happen because government was given too much power or citizen apathy. Because of government creep we now have the NSA spying on all Americans. Government now controls almost every aspect of our life. Congressional power has been passed on to the Executive Branch in the form of agencies.

The lowercase libertarian believes there are free market solutions to most of today's problems. With few exceptions it takes government much more money and time to do what the free market can accomplish for less.

We find many uppercase Libertarians who believe many of the problems lie with corporations. They even see the problem with mega corporation's marriage to government. The uppercase Libertarian will sometimes seek solutions through government. After the latest Wall Street crash we found many of these Libertarians within Occupy groups who sought more regulations. Increased regulation is growing government.

The lowercase libertarian would solve the problem by reducing regulation and government. If government hadn't had the power to create this government-finance partnership, the crash wouldn't have happened. Had the government not interfered in the housing market, this wouldn't have happened. Mortgage companies were forced by government to give loans they knew to be risky. In the end they were happy to make those loans because they could in turn sell them to quasi government entities such as Fannie Mae. Wall Street was all too happy to bundle these loans into securities and sell them worldwide.

If we look at how people see that one problem and their

solutions we can separate the lowercase libertarian from the uppercase Libertarian. If we add on social issues then we can clearly define all political groups. There is the Democratic Party, Republican Party, Conservatives, and the Libertarian Party. There are subtle differences that makes the lowercase libertarian an outcast in most groups. We know the Democratic party is progressive and for big government. In today's world there is little difference between the two major parties.

We then come to conservatives. At first look they appear similar to lowercase libertarians, but then we come to social issues. It's there they suddenly become big government oriented. They want government protectionism for such things as marriage, gambling, and drugs – just to list a few. Conservatives demands government legislate their brand of morality.

Then comes the Libertarian Party. It seems to be a mixed bag. It has true lowercase libertarians, but in the mix they have true communist who see the perfect society as being governed much like the Amish have for centuries. Add the Anarchist who want absolutely no government and you never know what will come next.

The lowercase libertarian has no party and will always be the outcast and forced to wear the extremist label. This is despite the fact we are less extreme than all the other groups. We believe people should be allowed to do stupid things as long as it doesn't harm others. It is the job of families to help those with addiction and other problems, not the government. Government imprisons addicts rather than treating them. Government too often prevents Americans from helping addicted family members.

But let's be sure legalization of drugs is not high on the list, it is often simply used as an example of how forced prohibition has never worked. The 21st Amendment is a testament to how prohibition fails.

The government ban of something has never worked. The only thing government bans accomplish is to drive up crime and increase market value. This is why the lowercase libertarian believes less government is usually the best solution. Because of New York City regulations on restaurants, they have created the underground diner.

For all the reasons above, it will be the lowercase libertarians that will save the world from itself. Any other course and we will live under tyranny, much worse than the one Americans live under today. We must choose the only road to liberty, the lowercase libertarian.

When is a Conservative liberal?

Published on
10/28/13 9:51 AM

We have political liberals and political conservatives. We can break this down to liberals wanting more government with conservatives wanting less. Yet in life we find many conservatives who are very liberal in their life. Many conservatives are smokers, while we have liberals who are for smoking bans.

A political liberal might be more the party type, while at the same time calling for stricter laws on alcohol. A political conservative might or might not be a partier. Both conservatives and liberals are guilty of calling for bans, although each might call for the ban of books or movies on opposite ends of the spectrum.

We can be sure a political liberal isn't always liberal thinking and a conservative isn't always conservative in how they live their life. Some see conservatives as people who spend their lives in church and are teetotalers. You would think they didn't smoke, wear short skirts, or expose cleavage, but we find many conservatives that do these things. Not all conservatives are social conservatives.

We find political liberals who are devout Christian who live very socially conservative lives. On the other end of the spectrum we find political liberals who spend much of their life partying, drinking, or using drugs. We should ask how can both groups be considered liberal? This can be answered by breaking down both political groups to interventionists and non-interventionists.

We have both socially conservative Democrats as well as liberal Democrats. For the other side we have socially conservative Republicans and fiscally conservative Republicans. Socially conservative republicans are against gay marriage, while socially conservative Democrats may or may not be for gay marriage, but are likely to at least be for civil unions. Fiscally conservative Republicans are also more likely to be for gay marriage or at least civil unions.

Are you finding this confusing? It often is. We find people who proudly wear the same label having different beliefs. We often find that some place labels on others that don't fit. Too often Republicans place the liberal label on Democrats when the progressive label is more fitting, while neither label accurately describes their beliefs. I think looking back few would find anything liberating or progressive about the Great Depression, yet that is the defining period in history for progressive Democrats.

No matter the political ideology we find both interventionists and non-interventionists. Can someone truly say they are for less government when they are interventionists? We cannot have it both ways. We cannot be for less government in some areas and more in others. Must we choose a side and be either interventionist or non-interventionist? I dare say few will fall completely in one category.

I do believe that if we are going to say we are for less

government we should strive to be non-interventionist whenever possible. No matter our political belief we should stop and look at every situation in the light of interventionist or non-interventionist. I believe if we do that we will often see the world in a different light. I personally have done that later in life, but never thought of it in these terms.

Who really wants government or the neighbor telling us how to live our lives? Sometimes even the homeless or the poor are happy with their lives. Recently I learned how the Supplemental Nutrition Assistance Program (SNAP) came into existence. When the federal government offered poor Appalachians foods stamps they refused because they were proud self-reliant people. When offered seeds the Appalachian farmers gladly accepted them. The government never to be denied, decided that if they tied food stamps to free seeds the poor farmers would be forced to accept them. The government was right, farmers accepted SNAP if it meant receiving new seed.

Forced intervention is the way of big government, no matter the label under which it was elected. No matter the party, we find those for big government. Today we have a government that too often sees itself helping whether we want it or not. Now I ask, do you want an interventionist or non-interventionist government?

Anarchical Societies vs Libertarianism

Published on
12/8/13 4:36 PM

Anarchist Utopian is an oxymoron if there ever was one – right? Maybe not as much as one thinks. Utopia was this fictional society where everything was perfect. Typically we think of communist or socialist societies as false Utopias. I think to expand the definition to any society that is filled with absolutes and infringes on the liberties of others.

We must ask. Can an Anarchical society that believes in absolute individual liberty infringe on the liberties of others? Any society that deals in absolutes forces their beliefs on others. To understand this we must understand why we have towns and cities. We can start this with "Once upon a time." Yes – we go that far back. The earliest humans were by nature social creatures. Unlike animals, they don't abandon their family once grown. Because of this nurturing instinct humans began to share common resources.

In time they found that forming close knit societies helped them survive the ravages of nature and enemies. As time went on and the small communities grew, they found that it helped if they selected a few to make some of the decisions for all. They would select villagers thought to be the wisest and most educated to make decisions for the community. People found they couldn't leave fields to vote on each small decision needed to be made. Of course there were some who didn't agree with the decisions and they would leave the community. They would sometimes form their own communities with a different set of rules. There was one thing all communities had in common, they had an individual or group making decisions for the collective.

We know communes such as the Amish have a group of elders to enforce societal rules. Another word for societal rule is law. The ones that aren't happy with their strict way of life move out of the community. No one is forced to live in their society, but if they choose to do so then they must follow strict rules.

Towns and cities are no different. Over the years people of these social communities have made laws by which people must abide. There are many who don't like the taxes and laws of cities and choose to live in the county. But even there you find laws and taxes. The reason there are taxes is the people decided it was more efficient to have a single purchasing body. We could just leave roads to be built by need by capitalist. Some believe that would work quite well. The only practical concept of this that comes to mind are housing developments and shopping centers. Even then residents must pay an annual fee to maintain those streets. Those fees are paid to some governmental body elected/appointed by the community. They pay that in conjunction with taxes needed to maintain streets built by the larger community/city.

For good or bad some people choose to allow government to make decisions for them. They agree to pay taxes to fund some of these decisions. This is a system that has been around for thousands of years. This system is often abused and an apathetic populous allows this abuse to continue. This doesn't make the system evil or unneeded.

In some societies there have been armed revolution to remove the abusive government. In others they have manged change through angry protests and occasionally the ballot box. When we are faced with an abusive government we have choices. We can do one of the above or we can simply move to a community or area that better suits how we wish to live.

It is obvious most people are content with a governmental society. If they weren't at least content there would be riots or violent revolution. If we wish to live in a community, but don't like how it functions we can work to effect change. Throughout history movements have created change, some good and bad. If we cannot effect change to our satisfaction we have the choice of moving or simply submitting to societal rules.

I get the impression that Anarchists don't want to move and wish to reform society to what they believe best. Some would choose armed revolt to change their community, while others just shout angrily at those who disagree. Anarchist could just move somewhere and start anew. I would love to see how a functioning anarchical society managed. I am sure of one thing, most people will not accept anarchy as a way of life.

This is my concern about Anarchists. If they force anarchy on everyone they have trampled the individual liberties of others. This is where a libertarians differ. We believe people have the right to be communist if that's their desire. We do not want to force anyone to do anything. We accept government has a place, but it must be held to a minimum. We accept communities can have rules, but kept to a minimum.

One Anarchist is angry her neighborhood is about to be annexed into the city. She feels her individual rights are being trampled. Many people have become angry at annexation. I would feel the same way. If enough neighbors help fight annexation it is sometimes defeated. If it can't be defeated there is only one other option – move.

The Anarchist must understand that individualism is fantastic, but it's not the only solution or choice. Revolutions aren't fought by individuals. They are fought by a collective under a central command. This is done for strength. An Anarchist cannot force their beliefs on others because they see that way of life as best. If they force this on others they are guilty of the same violations of individual rights as they claim to hate.

I fight the tyrannical federal government we have today. I see there are problems on the state and local levels as well. If we can return power to states we can then look inward to the problems there. I believe the Constitution is worth saving and restoring to its original functionality. Laws aren't evil, they are a part of any social community. It's when laws aren't applied equally that they become bad. We have this problem because people are either apathetic or they want government to enforce their personal prejudices.

There is one thing of which we can be sure, societal groups will always have rules. They will always find efficient ways to meet needs, even if that means pooling resources. We as a people must always be leery when allocating power to any group of people. The one thing history has taught us is that absolutes always turn out badly. Absolute anarchy is not Utopia, because perfection doesn't exist. Forcing Anarchy on others is as bad as forcing communism on everyone. Those are both ends of societal extremes.

Communism always fails. The wild west might be as close as we ever came to total anarchy. In time people began to coalesce into communities for a variety of reasons. There is a reason we have no anarchical societies, most people don't want them. I dream someday of a libertarian America, but if even that is done by force it's wrong. My only hope is to convince people that libertarianism is the best course and try to get those who share my beliefs voted into office.

Total anarchy would be the end to this country. I'm not sure many are ready for George Soros' Open Society. The libertarian doesn't always agree on how borders should operate, but we all have a love for this country. We believe in the original Constitution. For this reason I say no to total anarchy and accept that we are social creatures. I can still promote free market solutions to problems and fight to remove as much government from my life as possible. I will fight to make sure others don't use government to force their prejudices on others. I will fight for secession if that's the only way to achieve individual liberty and equality under the law. But at the moment I seek to save this country – not be a part of it's destruction. Total anarchy would make this just a patch of land with a lot of individuals running around doing as they please. I trust we can have a free market without having to resort to anarchy.

The hope of no authority is a pipe dream. We have all had parents telling us what to do. We have teachers and employers that we give some control over our lives. The only way to have total control over your life is to move to a mountain top. If you wish to live in an ordered society some control must be given to others.

T. L. Crain

Author note: *I should note this is more an observation on societal evolution than an opinion on Anarchism in any form. This is definitely not in support of government.*

Progressives Versus Corporations

Published on
11/30/13 12:25 PM

I recently had a day long twitter exchange with a progressive. As usual it always came down to the evils corporations do. Are there corporations that place profits over common morality? Of course. There are corporations doing things that can be seen as crimes against nature, but they typically do them in countries like China.

I tried explaining to the progressive that taxes and government regulations force these companies to move jobs to countries like China where sweat shops thrive. In some cases the poor in China are happy to have jobs even if they are in deplorable conditions. This isn't an excuse for consumers and corporations that ignore the plight of foreign workers – it's just one symptom of poverty and an out of control Chinese government.

In the USA we have a long list of jobs that the left calls, "Jobs Americans won't do." For those jobs we import workers from south of the border who are happy to have any job. Those people are so desperate for even the lowest paying American jobs that they sometimes risk their life coming to this country. This is despite such trade agreements like NAFTA that has driven American jobs across the southern border. NAFTA decimated many rural textile communities such as the one in which I live.

The progressive can find fault only in corporations that moved jobs, and none in the government that has control over laws and regulations. Progressives cry that corporations buy politicians. They are right, many politicians govern according to lobby and campaign monies. Of the two, corporations and politicians, we have only direct control over one, those that make up our government.

> *"Who deserves the most blame, – the temptress or the tempted?*
> *Blame falls fully on the shoulders of the one with whom the public has placed their trust."* –T.L. Crain

Many believe that term limits and campaign finance will help solve the corruption problems. It will do little. Term limits just make the elected work quicker to build their personal fortune. Finance control impinges on liberty and the right to freely participate in the election system.

There is no effective way to control power. A nuclear reactor doesn't control the power within, it simply either prevents its transformation or dissipates it in the form of heat. The only way to curb political power is to prevent its creation. There is currently no means to dissipate power in Washington. The founders knew the problems of a centralized power, and that's why they put in place a system that reserved most power for the states. The 17th Amendment that began the process of electing Senators took a large chunk of power from states.

There are many movements to transfer power from the federal government back to the states, but none have have drawn strong support from either political party. Repeal of the 17th Amendment is likely the most popular. Money is the root of all power. Until we remove that power from the federal government then all we will ever do is place band-aids over a bleeding artery. Death of liberty can be the only outcome if we continue the course. As it stands today, Nullification is the state's best weapon against federalism. A new option is the Freedom Tax amendment (Described in detail later) that removes taxing authority from the federal government and places it solely in state hands.

Each week we turn on the news to learn of another case of how the IRS has abused it's power against the Tea Party or some other political organization. The IRS should stand as the symbol of tyranny. Until the IRS is eliminated and that power taken from the Executive Branch, little will change. Whenever a group of citizens threaten to squash the central authority they will be silenced or discredited. The government will use its might and its control of the media to use the few bad apples in any group to tarnish the message and the movement. We must never forget that the existence of broadcast media is in the hands of the FCC, an arm of the Executive Branch.

We can ask government to pass more laws that will restrict cronyism between itself and corporations, but we all know each regulation has a loophole that can be used and abused. The relationship between government and banking has become legendary. We have only to look at the Federal Reserve Banking System to find cronyism at its greatest. On Jekyll Island the greatest plot ever to control the American economy was hatched. The Federal Reserve Act made taxation obsolete because whenever the government needs money it's simply created. This causes inflation – also known as the poor man's tax. Until the Federal Reserve system came along the US Treasury had to either print actual currency or sell bonds to create debt.

A progressive will never give a clear answer when asked for the best solution to ending cronyism. This is because they have none, other than to give government even more power and to pass even more useless regulations. We know from history that more government has rarely solved a problem. The progressive will talk in extremes and say people like me want no government. Any sensible person knows this to not be true. The founders maintained that the majority of power should be left with the states. Even states practice cronyism, but at least there they are forced to compete with other states for jobs. One act of cronyism doesn't effect an entire nation and it's global trade.

We learn politics through sports

Published on
9/2/13 1:02 AM

I came to realize last night while talking with a friend just how politics and sports are similar. I remember the day I stopped being a NASCAR fan. Dale Earnhardt had just wrecked and his car sat on the grass with flat tires. This accident should have put him out of contention because according to NASCAR rules the car would have to be towed to the garage area. It is only then the car can be worked on by the crew.

As the rollback truck backed up to the race car and began attaching the cable, Dale began shouting and frantically waving his arms. He stopped the track crewman from further actions, all the while shouting that loading the car would cause further damage.

Moments later Dale's pit crew appeared carrying tires and a jack. While in the infield grass they put tires on the car and Dale was soon back on the track three laps down. He came back to win the race while fans screamed loudly.

Some might wonder how this compares to politics, while some are smiling at this point. Because Earnhardt was extremely popular, NASCAR loved the money he made for them, and the sports media was all too happy to have a new king of racing, so they didn't push the extreme violation of rules. Any other driver would have been severely penalized during the race.

We see the same thing happening in the world of politics.

When you have a large segment of the population, a complicit media, certain politicians can get away with anything short of public homicide. President Obama has done things for which H.W. Bush and other presidents were demonized. Even the simple act of playing golf caused an uproar for Bush, while Obama plays much more often, and it's defended by the media.

Too many of us have been guilty of overlooking wrong doings as long as it is done by our own team. This state of mind seems to start with t-ball and continues all the way though professional sports. We all know of the home field advantage, which in part means officials will likely favor the home team. I don't see how we expect the world of politics to be any different. We have been taught since childhood to always support the home team. I see people who proudly state the fact that for several generations their family has always voted for the Democratic candidate. You find the same allegiance to unions. Many often resort to fisticuffs in support of the home team.

The first step in fixing this country and the government is to first look inward at our own actions. Will you be the first to step forward and complain when the umpire calls a clear strike a ball in favor of your own child?

Too many of us help cover and dismiss past and present mistakes of our own candidates and elected officials. Trends sometimes begin with one person. Will this new trend of doing the right thing start with you? The next time there is a clear violation of the Constitution, but it's in favor of your personal beliefs, will you complain?

Is The Political Left Evil?

Published on
1/6/11 6:57 PM

The Teatarian

Those of us that follow the political world tend to find any position other than our own, evil. So I ask, is the left evil? The clear answer is no. That doesn't mean that there isn't evil within all ideologies. I find most people have a good heart. They care about others. They worry about those without housing, food, and health-care. Those are not bad things.

What the left often gets wrong about the right, is that we worry about the same things. It's only how we wish to solve these problems that differs. We on the right believe that the poor are best severed when the rest prosper. Through the free-market system we have made the American poor some of the richest people in the world.

Those on the left run around shouting that the rich need to pay more. If we confiscated the wealth of anyone possessing more than a million dollars, we couldn't even pay off the current national debt.

I wonder how many people on the left would be willing to give up the simplest things so that the poor around the world could eat properly. If people were told that giving up cell phones would end world hunger and poverty, would they? I dare say they wouldn't.

On the other hand, are people on the right greedy? Sure, maybe some, but most humans are. What makes people on the political right different is they are realist. We know that confiscating wealth will do little to solve all the problems the left holds dear. Since the 50's we have each year put more and more money into education, yet test scores continue to drop.

What is evil, are the power mongers that will use the good hearts of people on the left to further political ambitions. For decades those in power on the left have been promising black Americans prosperity, yet it has never come. The best those of us on the right can promise anyone is equality under the law.

Leftist leaders tell their flock that people like Marx, Stalin, Hitler, and Mao all had the right idea, but were the wrong ones to build socialist and communist societies. Everyone that stands today declares they are the correct people to create the perfect socialist society.

We have learned from the past that power corrupts. That is why our founders created a government with separation of powers. It's the corruption of those powers that's the downfall of the greatest country ever on this world. The Executive branch is one step away from completely removing congressional power.

The left and right have to stop seeing the other as evil and look to what truly is evil. I believe those of us that are the Tea Party has managed to see the true evil. Evil is the traditional politician, no matter to which party they belong. Too much government is inherently evil.

America The Offended

Published on
12/14/13 9:27 AM

Everyday I face a world where I find person after person who is offended over this or that. The political right often points to the left as examples of those most using offensiveness. I find that no political ideology has a monopoly on being offended.

Missing graphic is a billboard with the word 'Christ' crossed out that reads, "Who needs Christ in Christmas? Nobody."

Eric Bolling of Fox News interviewed the head of an Atheist organization and repeatedly stated how he was offended by the billboard described above. It's fair to state when you are offended by something, even though the billboard wasn't directed at Bolling personally. It becomes hypocritical when you often demand others not be offended. Free speech demands we have a thick skin and stop being offended by another person's free expression.

This is no different from the attacks on Megyn Kelly for saying that Santa Claus was white. The origins of the jolly fat man comes from the Nordic culture. Sorry, but those people were and are white. Santa has been depicted as white since the jolly old man's inception. This doesn't mean you can't have a black, Indian, or Arabian Santa. It's a free country, decorate your home as you please. Have whatever Santa you want in your places of gathering. What must stop is being offended and using offensiveness to attack others.

Religion, holidays, flesh color, heritage, lifestyle, and many other things are being used to divide us for political and profitable gain. We are all forced to live on this ball of rock and must find ways to get along. I have spent hours watching Atheists and Christians argue over who is correct. It's insanity to believe either person is going to change their mind. Belief or non-belief isn't wrong as long as it's not used to do harm, or is forced on another. Each have reasons for strongly embracing their belief or non-belief.

Those in government will use our social differences against us in an effort to gain power. Some days I feel we never left high school where we were divided by differences with Jocks on one side of the hall and academics on the other. There were the hooligans in one section with geeks in another. A few of us somehow managed to find acceptance in every group. I found there were the different groups because they formed prejudices about those in other groups. If you held no prejudices you could move between social groups.

I hold no prejudices for Christian, Atheist, Muslim, or LGBT. But I do have prejudices against individual actions. In every group mentioned there are those who are filled with prejudice and attack others for not being accepting of their belief or lifestyle. No amount of shouting and anger is going to make anyone accept you, your beliefs, or lifestyle. No law will end prejudice. We must all look inward and think before we speak ill of another simply because of their beliefs or lifestyle. This is the greatest part of being American, we can believe or live our lives as we see fit. No amount of hate and anger will make those for whom we have prejudices disappear. We must at times close our eyes and walk past the things for which we have prejudices.

When we turn to government and ask it to legislate in favor of our belief or lifestyle we are opening the door for tyranny. The current government might use the power given in support of our personal prejudices. The next government might favor those for whom we have prejudices and you suddenly find yourself on the bottom.

German Jews and Japanese-Americans embraced and empowered their governments and were later imprisoned. The patriotic current can change at any moment and send us crashing into the rocks. Beware of the power given to others over you. We often give government power over us and later find ourselves filled with regret. When we become offended we are giving power over us because they know then words can be used as a weapon.

The world in which we live and the one filled with politics are much the same. Social groups can be as political in nature as if you were on the Capitol floor. I speak often of the Dog And Pony Show (DAPS) and when we become offended by the speech of others we become a part of the show. Being offended is one of the greatest political tools ever devised. Stop being a part of DAPS and look for areas in which you agree so that we can work together in an effort to rein in an out of control central government. If you must be offended at something let it be the arrogant government in Washington.

Today, the only groups for which it's acceptable to poke fun are those who live in trailers or the Appalachian Mountains. Terms such as hillbilly and trailer trash are tossed around as the butt of many jokes. As a southern rural person who once lived in a trailer park and might be considered trailer trash, I could take offense. I don't because I know it's often in jest. When it is intended as a derogatory statement I simply refuse to give that person power over me. It is they who must live with their ignorance – not me.

A Push for fewer children

Published on
8/7/13 6:26 PM

Let's begin this by saying that life should hold no mandate to have children. Now that's out of the way, let's add the 'but.' I wrote previously how the progressive agenda is being driven by the environmentalists and the population control crowd. I see no problem in having no children, since that was my choice in life. I didn't do it because of some environmental concern, or for career paths, it was just a personal decision.

We, at times, see the choice of having no children glorified. As someone who made that choice, there are times of regret for having made that decision. If I could turn back time, that might be one of the many different choices in my life.

My point is that we must make these decisions based on what we feel is best for ourselves at the time. From someone who made the no children decision, I warn you to not listen to the progressive and environmentalist voices. One can propose many logical reasons to have or not have children.

Imagine you are staring in the mirror at your gray hair and having regrets about your no child decision. You now know that you could have had a successful career and children—you realize the catastrophe of climate change never happened and never would have happened no matter your decision.

From 2007 to 2011, the most recent year for which there is

data, the fertility rate declined 9%. A 2010 Pew Research report showed that childlessness had risen across all racial and ethnic groups, adding up to about 1 in 5 American women who had passed their childbearing years. This trend doesn't seem to be changing. We can attribute some of this to lifestyle changes. We have so many distractions that sometimes it can be hard to find time for activities that lead to having children. Some of this can be due to better pregnancy prevention.

No one can predict the future and say that having fewer children will be beneficial or harmful. Some even look at statistics with a xenophobic view. Whatever the reason for not having children, or just having one, it must be your decision.

Every day we are bombarded with information and opinions that run the board. One thing is sure, humans will procreate. Because of World War II there was a baby boom as soldiers returned home. The great depression had ended and people could afford to have children. Socioeconomic conditions have always had an effect on the rate of childbirths.

Because of the high rate of divorces and the large number of single mothers we know that in the end childbirth must be the woman's decision. Make it for your own reasons and block out political influences.

"The government always has"

Published on
8/19/13 7:17 PM

Frequently we hear people say, "The government has always done it this way." When we hear that we should stop and take pause. That statement alone exemplifies the problems in this country. We have reached a time when the Constitution no longer matters and government picks and chooses which laws to enforce.

I was recently told that we should support flawed Bills and that the Executive Branch has always picked and chosen which laws they enforced. The argument for the latter was there are only so many resources and they must be allocated according to need.

If we have more laws than can be enforced, then that should tell us one thing – we need less laws or more enforcement. Enforcement is expensive, so that leaves only one thing, which is to have less laws to enforce. Statistics show we imprison more people per capita than almost any country in the world. Many of these incarcerations are drug related. Too often violent criminals are freed through early parole in order to make room for drug offenders.

No matter whether you are for drug legalization or not, the country has reached a crisis point. Enforcement doesn't have the manpower to sometimes go after potential terrorists who entered the country illegally. We have Justice Department officials deciding which laws to enforce, and too often that decision is guided by political and ideological beliefs.

We cannot continue with business as usual. Every state in the country decides drug laws. We do not need this duplicated on the federal level except when the illegal activity crosses state lines. Federal agents should then only enforce the laws of the state in which the violation occurred.

Let's look at how laws against marijuana first came to exist. Hemp at the time was the most popular source of marijuana. Hemp was used for making rope. In the 60's a common term for smoking marijuana was "smoking rope." For two years Congress secretly deliberated until if finally passed the Marihuana Tax Stamp Act of 1937. The first serious regulation of marijuana was 1906, in Washington DC. By 1930, sixteen states had banned the use of marijuana except for medicinal purposes.

The push to ban cocaine and opium (and later marijuana) at the federal level ran into a serious obstacle, the Tenth

Amendment to the United States Constitution, which said powers not delegated to the federal government through the Constitution were reserved for the states. The federal government would not be denied and used taxes and regulation to control the use of marijuana and other drugs. In 1969 the Marijuana Tax Stamp Act of 1937 was found to be unconstitutional. Once again the federal government refused to be denied power and the U.S. Congress responded by passing The Controlled Substances Act in 1970, citing "interstate commerce" as the basis for its authority. The U.S. Supreme Court recognized the so-called "commerce clause" to uphold a series of laws that effectively gutted the Tenth Amendment's reservation of rights to the states. The commerce clause has been used to literally gut the Constitution.

Look at what all these federal drug laws have given us. We have essentially created a police state. Combine the war on drugs with the war on terrorism, and the federal government has become far reaching. Today we face laws such as Stop and Frisk and NSA spying. I can assure you, those are not things the government has always done."

Until Americans stop settling for politicians who lie, a government that constantly talks protectionism, while passing flawed laws, things will get only worse. The next time someone says, "the government always has," ask them why and then remind them the government "hasn't always." Edward Bernays taught government how to fool the public into accepting things they wouldn't want otherwise. Bernays is the father of propaganda and marketing.

Many Americans are so desperate for change they jump on the bandwagon of anyone promising change. Obama was elected twice on the promise of change. People are excited about Mark Levin and his convention of the states that seeks to pass unexplained amendments.

Politicians want only power and money. Too many television and radio personalities seek only fame and money.

There are political groups that seek only money. We must find people who truly care and are willing to listen to average America – who can push a real agenda of well thought out change. The government hasn't always.

Voting "None of the Above"

Published on
11/30/13 12:20 PM

Jack, a member of America Chooses, had a fantastic idea. He suggested that on all election ballots we add another option, "None of the above." I've been giving that some thought and came up with a few ideas on how this could be done effectively.

If "None of the above" receives the most votes then the law should state that a new election be held within six months, or possibly the next year, and that none of the candidates in the previous election would be eligible to run. In the mean time, the governor or state assembly would select an acting US Representative or Senator, or whatever the office may be. In the second election "None of the above" likely wouldn't be on the ballot.

We could possible use this to at least temporarily override the 17th Amendment and have the state legislature appoint the Senator. It might be possible to always have "None of the above" on the Senate ballot. That would leave the power to circumvent the 17th Amendment in the voters' hands.

This doesn't make it perfect, but it at least pushes out the party favorites that no one likes. This could also work for other elections as well. On the county or city level the mayor or council could choose an acting office holder until the next election could be held.

I would love for something like this in primaries, but for

45

presidential races it would be impossible to wait for the next year and would be a financial burden to hold another election within a few months. Also primaries are held by the parties and they can make their own rules. We could at least push for this idea within our own parties.

I think Jack is like myself and tired of poor choices come election time. Look at past elections where we ended up with presidential candidates like John McCain and Mitt Romney. Over and over we see the same people running in elections. We find that party bigwigs tend to get their way. Jack's solution isn't perfect, but it's a start. We need new blood in elections. This would help us weed out those who make a career of holding the same office.

Another problem that faces us are filing fees required to run for office. The average person can't afford these fees. People might look to start an independent group through which they raise capital, put in place a minimum set of standards for candidates, and pay filing fees for those who meet that criteria. We have got to do something to get fresh blood on the ballots. Business as usual is no longer adequate.

We have got to start thinking out of the box. We must make it easier for independents to hold office. For too long we have been accepting rules set by the power players. It's time we change the rules and put power back in the people's hands. As long as we remain sheep we will be susceptible to political wolves.

Give us your suggestions. We need everyone's help to change the system and make it work better for the people, not just the power brokers.

Winning America through education

Published on
9/27/13 9:48 AM

Too frequently I find myself in debates with the typical Democratic voter and they will repeat the same rhetoric they get from peers and the 6pm news. Five minutes into the conversation they have the doe in the headlight look. Once I begin explaining basic finance and use words like Quantitative Easing and Rehypothification, they run away.

If they do stick around past that point, the moment I mention the free market they point to what they believe are faults in capitalism. They tell me how it was capitalism that caused the crash of 2007, and how the greedy bankers are taking people's homes. They tell me how companies like Monsanto are poisoning everyone. I could go on, but you get the message. Everyone knows all the arguments.

I must then explain to these people we have not had a free market in modern history. Not since *Wikard versus Filburn* have we come close to a free market. This opened the door for federal regulation of almost everything produced in America. All the problems mentioned above, and then some, are done with cooperation from the overseer government.

The average person believes the solution to all market problems is more regulation. This is despite the fact there are already regulations in place that's suppose to protect the employee or consumer. I find it almost impossible to explain how government is often a part of the problem and rarely the solution.

Let's drift back to 2007 once more when the housing bubble began deflating. Many people who consider themselves the educated and informed will point to the weakening of Glass-Steagall as the root cause. In a sense they are correct. If Glass-Steagall had remained intact that would have kept banks more stable. This thinking is the same as a doctor treating only the symptoms of a terminal illness.

Preventing the problems that caused the 2007 decline would have been the better solution. The root cause of the

2007 economic collapse was government interfering in the housing market. Since the 70's government has been forcing lending institutions to give mortgages to people who were higher risk. In 1998 Clinton increased the number of people who qualified for mortgages. Then came the normal downturn in the economy.

Because mortgage holders were living on the edge and then had working hours cut back, or they were laid off, they could no longer make payments. Banks then began foreclosing. Then came a government created problem. The government had allowed, and in some cases forced, lending institutions to sell those mortgages to securities companies. They bundled those high risk mortgages and sold them at premium prices. As home owners defaulted the securities that held their mortgages began to drastically lose value. This sent economic ripples around the world.

It's clear to those of us that looked deeply into the crisis that the free market wasn't at fault, but its manipulation by government. The economic cycle is a sine wave, a line that curves up and down. Progressives believe they can make the economic line straight, by removing ups and downs. The Great Depression is a perfect example of their attempts at controlling the economy.

Life won't be perfect under a true free market economy, but it's not under the current system. I, and many like me, ask only that a true free market economy be given a chance. One cannot say that a free market doesn't work because it hasn't been tried in this country, or any other that comes to mind. This doesn't mean removing all regulations from the market, at least on the state and local level. Almost all federal regulation will have to be dismissed. The free market always fights for survival. In the USA and around the world we find the the underground market being the freest.

And they came for the children

Published on
11/28/12 2:54 PM

You cannot find a Republican source that isn't trying to define why they lost the 2012 presidential election. All logic dictates that with 8% unemployment, Obama should have lost, except he didn't. The loss was an electoral landslide, while the popular vote was close.

The only thing that matters at this point is the loss. Romney was a weak candidate, but he was portrayed as the only man that could beat Obama. What republicans don't understand is it doesn't matter if the candidate is good or bad. Most people vote with their feelings.

After Tropical Storm Sandy hit and we saw Governor Christie parading Obama around telling us what a fantastic job he was doing, people sitting on the fence fell to Obama's side. They felt he cared. It's not even important if he did care, it's the fact that he projected that image.

Republicans fail to see that politics is no different from American Idol. It doesn't matter how well you can sing, it's all about if you are liked and have some sob story. Romney grew up wealthy, while Obama grew up in perceived poverty. Obama's every word was about helping the poor and middle class. Romney's mistake was that he thought logically. He had the same concerns, but he was going about solving the problem logically. Most people are confused by a logical mind – it doesn't matter if you are on the left or the right.

The average person can't see that reducing regulations and lowering taxes for business will stimulate the economy and provide more jobs and a better life for the poor and middle class. We have educated democrats telling people that supply-side economics can't work, when in fact it has worked everywhere it's been tried. If people took the time to study the history of Chile, or look at the real numbers of the Reagan era, they would see it works.

Most voters are not going to look at these things. They want to vote for the cutest or the one that can give them the warm fuzzies when they speak. Charisma will win over logic every time. Ronald Reagan didn't win because he had some great economic ideas. He won because he was more likeable than the other candidate.

Right now the Republican Party has a branding problem. Many people see this as the party for big business. They cannot fathom the economic principles on which it's based. Republican candidates rarely defend themselves against the lies of opponents. They seem to feel they can win on messaging alone. This just doesn't work.

Republicans have a firm foothold in the south, but even that is beginning to slip. If we look back a few short decades, the south was predominately democrat. Until the 60's southern people were still believers in the FDR myth. Some want to blame the shift on the civil rights movement. I have no doubt that played some part, but that wasn't the principle item. Things changed after Kennedy was killed. The Democratic party took a sharp left turn left with the seating of President Johnson.

In the south we have a distrust of government, especially the US government. Our ancestors watched their homes burned and neighbors imprisoned simply because of their political beliefs. Most southerners didn't care in which country they lived, they just wanted a chance to live free and without worry.

The point I'm making is that the democrats aren't controlling some states because of their actions, they are winning because of who they are perceived to be. The war on poverty is a good example. Unemployment and income levels of blacks is no different from the 70's when the war on poverty began. It's only the perception of democrats caring, and their handing out free stuff, that matters.

Today our schools are mostly run by progressives. They take the minds of our young children and mold them into future progressives. Unless conservatives and libertarians want to become a thing of the past, they must take control of the education system. This cannot happen until we take back control of education from Washington DC.

Republicans must find a way to make people believe they don't want to imprison gays and adulterers. This sounds absurd, right? But this is the perception by many people. The left is controlling the message. Many republican voters are libertarian or Teatarian minded people. That is why it's going to be up to us to help take over the messaging. We must drag social conservatives kicking and screaming to the side where people should be allowed to live their personal lives as they choose. We must make them understand that government has no business controlling marriage in any form. We must reduce the control of government in our lives, both financial and social.

Knowing History—The Pledge of Allegiance

Published on
9/19/13 9:42 AM

The Pledge of Allegiance is something I thought little about as I stood in my grammar school class each day repeating the phrase. My only thoughts were that my nation was something about which to take great pride. I feel no differently today. The only difference today is that I often have to seek out corrections to history as taught by our schools and perpetuated by the different political ideologies. The simple Pledge of Allegiance is one of those things.

Where did the pledge originate?

The Pledge of Allegiance was written in August 1892 by the socialist, Baptist minister, Francis Bellamy (1855-1931). It was originally published in *The Youth's Companion* on September 8, 1892. Bellamy had hoped the pledge would be used by citizens in any country. Years after the Civil War had ended, the nation was still divided. This was an attempt to bring the nation together under one flag.

The pledge in its original form:
I pledge allegiance to my Flag and the Republic for which it stands, one nation, indivisible, with liberty and justice for all."

It was not until 1932 that the pledge was changed to specify the United States of America:

"I pledge allegiance to the Flag of the United States of America and to the Republic for which it stands, one nation, indivisible, with liberty and justice for all."

In 1954 President Eisenhower pushed congress to add 'under God' in response to the godless communist threat. This led to the pledge used today, and repeated by me in the first grade. I had lived most of my life never knowing the origins of the pledge I blindly repeated.

I pledge allegiance to the flag of the United States of America, and to the republic for which it stands, one nation under God, indivisible, with liberty and justice for all."

Section 4 of the Flag Code states:
The Pledge of Allegiance to the Flag: "I pledge allegiance to the Flag of the United States of America, and to the Republic for which it stands, one Nation under God,

indivisible, with liberty and justice for all.", should be rendered by standing at attention facing the flag with the right hand over the heart. When not in uniform men should remove any non-religious headdress with their right hand and hold it at the left shoulder, the hand being over the heart. Persons in uniform should remain silent, face the flag, and render the military salute."

Bellamy's salute, first described in 1892, began with the military salute at the beginning of the pledge. After citing the pledge the hand was to be extended up and outstretched toward the flag. We might better recognize the action as being similar to the Nazi salute. For this reason the salute was changed after World War II to simply place the right hand over the heart and maintaining it there until the pledge's end. For military the arm extension was eliminated.

From the Youth's Companion, 1892:

At a signal from the Principal the pupils, in ordered ranks, hands to the side, face the Flag. Another signal is given; every pupil gives the flag the military salute — right hand lifted, palm downward, to a line with the forehead and close to it. Standing thus, all repeat together, slowly, "I pledge allegiance to my Flag and the Republic for which it stands; one Nation indivisible, with Liberty and Justice for all." At the words, "to my Flag," the right hand is extended gracefully, palm upward, toward the Flag, and remains in this gesture till the end of the affirmation; whereupon all hands immediately drop to the side.

We must know our history accurately and never blindly follow. We should proudly honor the flag and the things for which it stands. But we must know that the pledge as it stands today was originally written by a Utopian socialist and has evolved over the years for various reasons.

Today there is an ideological war waging between Marxist-socialists and free market, constitutional-libertarians. This war has been raging since the nation's inception. There are clear periods where the Marxist-socialists had a winning advantage. The best known was in 1913 when the Federal Reserve came into existence – another when Franklin D. Roosevelt led, and maintained, the Great Depression.

The 60's brought us the wars on drugs and poverty – both problems are worse than ever today. We can find no period in history where Marxist-socialist policies have worked. The outcome is always the same, abject poverty. Today Marxist-socialists go by a different name. Today we know them as progressives. Progressives maintain a seat in all of today's political parties.

A Look at The Gettysburg Address

Published on
11/30/13 12:22 PM

Today is the anniversary of Lincoln's Gettysburg Address. Many see this speech as a great day in history, but every story has two sides. President Obama is being slammed for not mentioning God in his recitation. The reason could be simple, be chose one of the versions that didn't include the word 'God.'

I'd like to add a little commentary before listing the different versions below. Some of us don't see the Gettysburg Address as something great. Some of us in the south never saw this as a civil war. From the southern perspective it was an attack from another nation. I bring this up because either by force or choice we are today all Americans and we must always remember this period in history isn't always seen with the northern perspective.

Some might ask why this is important. The very words of Lincoln tell us why this is a topic that needs discussion, especially in today's turbulent political environment. He said, "a new nation, conceived in Liberty," We must understand the meaning of liberty. True liberty is the right to secede. If states lose the right to secede there can never be true liberty. For a state held at the point of a gun there is no true liberty. This was no different than attacking nations in order to force our brand of democracy on them.

Today we have states threatening to divide, at least one seceding and joining Canada. There are others with threats of secession. If any of these secessions come about, will more people die while trying to achieve true liberty? Will the heavy hand of the US government use armed force to stop the will of the people?

We sometimes get caught up in the moment and don't stop to look objectively at historical events. We know history is often written by the victor. The people in England still think of Americans as colonist. American patriots were guilty of treason in England. Each event has many sides. Each issue is complex. There are no simple solutions for our problems, but we must stop playing political games and try working together in an effort to solve problems. Obama not mentioning 'God' in the Gettysburg Address is a distraction, one we cannot afford at this time. We need to bring people together if we want to defeat the progressives in coming elections.

The Gettysburg Address

Gettysburg, Pennsylvania November 19, 1863

Bliss Copy

Ever since Lincoln wrote it in 1864, this version has been the most often reproduced, notably on the walls of the Lincoln Memorial in Washington. It is named after Colonel Alexander Bliss, stepson of historian George Bancroft. Bancroft asked President Lincoln for a copy to use as a fundraiser for soldiers (see "Bancroft Copy" below). However, because Lincoln wrote on both sides of the paper, the speech could not be reprinted, so Lincoln made another copy at Bliss's request. It is the last known copy written by Lincoln and the only one signed and dated by him. Today it is on display at the Lincoln Room of the White House.

Four score and seven years ago our fathers brought forth on this continent, a new nation, conceived in Liberty, and dedicated to the proposition that all men are created equal.
Now we are engaged in a great civil war, testing whether that nation, or any nation so conceived and so dedicated, can long endure. We are met on a great battle-field of that war. We have come to dedicate a portion of that field, as a final resting place for those who here gave their lives that that nation might live. It is altogether fitting and proper that we should do this.

But, in a larger sense, we can not dedicate -- we can not consecrate -- we can not hallow -- this ground. The brave men, living and dead, who struggled here, have consecrated it, far above our poor power to add or detract. The world will little note, nor long remember what we say here, but it can never forget what they did here. It is for us the living, rather, to be dedicated here to the unfinished work which they who fought here have thus far so nobly advanced. It is rather for us to be here dedicated to the great task remaining before us -- that from these honored dead we take increased devotion to that cause for which they gave the last full measure of devotion -- that we here highly resolve that these dead shall not have died in vain -- that this nation, under God, shall have a new birth of freedom -- and that government of the people, by the people, for the people, shall not perish from the earth.

Abraham Lincoln November 19, 1863

Nicolay Copy

Named for John G. Nicolay, President Lincoln's personal secretary, this is considered the "first draft" of the speech, begun in Washington on White house stationery. The second page is written on different paper stock, indicating it was finished in Gettysburg before the cemetery dedication began. Lincoln gave this draft to Nicolay, who went to Gettysburg with Lincoln and witnessed the speech. The Library of Congress owns this manuscript.

Four score and seven years ago our fathers brought forth, upon this continent, a new nation, conceived in liberty, and dedicated to the proposition that "all men are created equal."
Now we are engaged in a great civil war, testing whether that nation, or any nation so conceived, and so dedicated, can long endure. We are met on a great battle field of that war. We come to dedicate a portion of it, as a final resting place for those who died here, that the nation might live. This we may, in all propriety do.

But, in a larger sense, we can not dedicate – we can not consecrate – we can not hallow, this ground – The brave men, living and dead, who struggled here, have hallowed it, far above our poor power to add or detract. The world will little note, nor long remember what we say here; while it can never forget what they did here.

It is rather for us, the living, we here be dedicated to the great task remaining before us – that, from these honored dead we take increased devotion to that cause for which they here, gave the last full measure of devotion – that we here highly resolve these dead shall not have died in vain; that the nation, shall have a new birth of freedom, and that government of the people, by the people, for the people, shall not perish from the earth.

Hay Copy

Believed to be the second draft of the speech, President Lincoln gave this copy to John Hay, a White House assistant. Hay accompanied Lincoln to Gettysburg and briefly referred to the speech in his diary: "the President, in a fine, free way, with more grace than is his wont, said his half dozen words of consecration." The Hay copy, which includes Lincoln's handwritten changes, also is owned by the Library of Congress.

Four score and seven years ago our fathers brought forth, upon this continent, a new nation, conceived in Liberty, and dedicated to the proposition that all men are created equal.
Now we are engaged in a great civil war, testing whether

that nation, or any nation so conceived, and so dedicated, can long endure. We are met here on a great battlefield of that war. We have come to dedicate a portion of it, as a final resting place for those who here gave their lives that that nation might live. It is altogether fitting and proper that we should do this.

But in a larger sense, we can not dedicate — we can not consecrate — we can not hallow — this ground. The brave men, living and dead, who struggled here, have consecrated it far above our poor power to add or detract. The world will little note, nor long remember, what we say here, but can never forget what they did here. It is for us, the living, rather to be dedicated here to the unfinished work which they have, thus far, so nobly carried on. It is rather for us to be here dedicated to the great task remaining before us — that from these honored dead we take increased devotion to that cause for which they gave the last full measure of devotion – that we here highly resolve that these dead shall not have died in vain; that this nation shall have a new birth of freedom; and that this government of the people, by the people, for the people, shall not perish from the earth.

Everett Copy

Edward Everett, the chief speaker at the Gettysburg cemetery dedication, clearly was impressed by Lincoln's remarks and wrote to him the next day saying, "I should be glad, if I could flatter myself that I came as near to the central idea of the occasion, in two hours, as you did in two minutes." In 1864 Everett asked Lincoln for a copy of the speech to benefit Union soldiers, making it the third manuscript copy. Eventually the state of Illinois acquired it, where it's preserved at the Abraham Lincoln Presidential Library and Museum.

Four score and seven years ago our fathers brought forth, upon this continent, a new nation, conceived in Liberty, and dedicated to the proposition that all men are created equal.

Now we are engaged in a great civil war, testing whether that nation, or any nation so conceived, and so dedicated, can long endure. We are met on a great battle-field of that war. We have come to dedicate a portion of that field, as a final resting-place for those who here gave their lives, that that nation might live. It is altogether fitting and proper that we should do this.

But, in a larger sense, we can not dedicate, we can not consecrate — we can not hallow — this ground. The brave men, living and dead, who struggled here, have consecrated it far above our poor power to add or detract. The world will little note, nor long remember what we say here, but it can never forget what they did here.

It is for us, the living, rather, to be dedicated here to the unfinished work which they who fought here, have, thus far, so nobly advanced. It is rather for us to be here dedicated to the great task remaining before us — that from these honored dead we take increased devotion to that cause for which they here gave the last full measure of devotion — that we here highly resolve that these dead shall not have died in vain — that this nation, under God, shall have a new birth of freedom — and that government of the people, by the people, for the people, shall not perish from the earth.

Bancroft Copy

As noted above, historian George Bancroft asked President Lincoln for a copy to use as a fundraiser for soldiers. When Lincoln sent his copy on February 29, 1864, he used both sides of the paper, rendering the manuscript useless for lithographic engraving. So Bancroft kept this copy and Lincoln had to produce an additional one (Bliss Copy). The Bancroft copy is now owned by Cornell University.

Four score and seven years ago our fathers brought forth, on this continent, a new nation, conceived in Liberty, and dedicated to the proposition that all men are created equal.

Now we are engaged in a great civil war, testing whether that nation, or any nation so conceived, and so dedicated, can long endure. We are met on a great battle-field of that war. We have come to dedicate a portion of that field, as a final resting-place for those who here gave their lives, that that nation might live. It is altogether fitting and proper that we should do this.

But, in a larger sense, we can not dedicate, we can not consecrate — we can not hallow — this ground. The brave men, living and dead, who struggled here, have consecrated it far above our poor power to add or detract. The world will little note, nor long remember what we say here, but it can never forget what they did here. It is for us the living, rather, to be dedicated here to the unfinished work which they who fought here have thus far so nobly advanced. It is rather for us to be here dedicated to the great task remaining before us

– that from these honored dead we take increased devotion to that cause for which they here gave the last full measure of devotion - that we here highly resolve that these dead shall not have died in vain – that this nation, under God, shall have a new birth of freedom, and that government of the people, by the people, for the people, shall not perish from the earth.

Source for all versions: Collected Works of Abraham Lincoln, edited by Roy P. Basler and others.

Economics

Economics – Chickens, Cows, and Money

Published on
1/12/14 5:40 PM

People place a lot of importance on money, which is understandable. Bartering was once the major method of payment. In some eras something as simple as salt or spices were worth more than gold. The more rare an object the more its worth in comparison to other goods and services. The more rare the tradesmen, the greater their worth.

People can't provide everything they need for themselves. Let's say that a farmer needs a cow for milk. The cow cost ten chickens. Most cows are raised in a different village so the farmer has to haul the ten chickens to that village for trade. Most times he takes 11 chickens because one might die on the way.

Someone decided a long time ago that gold coins were a lot easier to carry around. One gold coin is worth 10 chickens. The farmer doesn't need a wagon to carry a single gold coin with which to buy the cow. He simply sold ten chickens to a village that was closer. Sounds pretty simple doesn't it? Well it was until the bankers came along.

You see, the bankers love gold. They buy gold and sometimes charge others to store it in a vault. They sometimes have so much gold it's not worth much. In the banker village a cow is still worth ten chickens, but it takes 10 gold coins to buy a cow. That doesn't matter too much except the bankers need chickens and they are so busy making gold coins they don't spend much time raising cows and chickens. They usually buy everything they need.

Eventually all the towns with which the bankers traded, the value of gold decreased because people began to have so much. This excess of gold eventually spread out to all villages until the day came when the farmer would need 10 gold coins to buy that cow, even though the cow is still worth 10 chickens. This leads to new problem.

Ranchers produce most of the cows in the area. Ranchers wanted more gold so they started producing more cows. Soon they were overflowing with cows. They eventually had to start selling the cows for 5 chickens just to get rid of them. All the villagers began to buy up cows until everyone had all they needed. The value of cows dropped to almost nothing. In the end, ranchers had the same amount of gold that they would have had if cow production had never been increased.

The same thing kind of happened with the bankers. They kept making gold coins until gold was nearly worthless. Eventually it would take hundreds of gold coins to buy chickens because the chicken farmers never over produced. When there is too much of one thing its value drops.

People of today often do the same thing. The government makes the paper you trade for stuff. Paper has no inherent value, but society has placed value on paper with certain words. That's kind of okay except when government makes too much of that paper. We could say one paper is worth ten chickens. You might think that the government could just make all the paper money it wants and people would have lots of paper to buy chickens. It's much like the bankers and gold. Too much of anything drops its value.

Countries all around the world produce their own paper. It would be silly for them to trade their paper equally with American paper because the government is printing so much. For the printed paper to have a fixed value it must also have a fixed quantity.

The government gives farmers printed paper in order not

to plant something. The government decides they want corn to be more expensive so they give farmers printed paper not to plant corn. Because beans were too expensive and in short supply, government began paying other farmers to plant beans to raise the quantity.

It looks to me that government is like some of the bad kings of old. They told people how to live. It is easy to control people when you control the food supply and the printed paper or gold supply. People were meant to be free creatures, but government enslaves them. As long as government controls the economy, it controls the people.

Basic economics is very simple. Government wants people to believe it's something only a massive bureaucracy can understand and control. If we look back to some societies of old we will notice everyone worked for the king – the land owner. Farmers and shop keepers kept what the king didn't take. Kings were notorious for giving land or loaning armies to friends and those who could do favors in return. In some places hunting animals for food was reserved only for royalty. The government of today greatly resembles the kings of old.

Government Controlled Economics – A Failure

Published on
3/1/14 2:59 PM

With the US economy trying to dig its way out of what has been erroneously called the Great Recession – we sit and watch the happenings in Washington. We recently heard a speech by the president reaffirming his desire to defeat climate change. Carbon emissions seem to be the number one item on the Washington agenda. While Congress sleeps the EPA and other agencies expand their regulatory power.

The American people elected a president who promised to

destroy the coal industry. He has the desire to make the coal industry a thing of the past. While use of coal in the USA has dropped, exports to Europe were up 92% in 2010-11, according to Platts. Electrical rates are expected to increase dramatically because of mandates for closing coal powered generation plants. The president said, "Electrical rates will necessarily dramatically increase." This is all in the name of saving the planet from climate warming that isn't currently happening and was never proven to be mostly caused by humans.

How many of you have taken a cruise? If so, how many of them flew the American flag? There is only one cruise ship operating under American registration, the American Pride. The reasons are simple that this profitable industry operates offshore – US regulations. These regulations are wide spread – everything from labor laws, environmental regulations, to health inspections.

If anyone wishes to see America's future they have only to look at the cruise industry. If government regulations can destroy one popular American pastime from operating within our own borders, they can do the same for many others.

In the past we watched the US government, because of pressure from environmental lobby groups, nearly destroy the nuclear power industry. For the most part of half a century no new nuclear power plant licenses were granted. With the government forced demise of coal powered electrical generation and the failure of wind and solar to become an adequate replacement – government and the environmental lobby have changed their minds when it comes to nuclear power. Nuclear energy that was once decried as evil is now the savior.

The point is to say that government has a poor record of picking winners and losers. Solyndra solar company has become the banner of government failing to pick winners. We are told over and over how the free market has failed. Few realize there has not been a free market in this country since the days of the wild west where there was little or no government.

People confuse cronyism with the free market. We have a government that is easily bought and sold by corporations and public lobby groups. It is impossible to say at this time one is more dangerous than the other. We have the environmental lobby that has dramatically increased gasoline prices – because of ethanol mandates – and nearly destroyed the nuclear power industry. We have the corporate lobby that buys government in order to create monopolies.

When is the last time you had to deal with one of these corporations? If you have you will find that many have grown so large that they have become terribly inefficient and customer unfriendly. It is rare when you can call one of these companies and talk to a human, and when you finally do we find they are incompetent. This is in part due to government created monopolies. Because the mom and pop business cannot afford to buy regulations and subsidies, they can never grow beyond a certain point. When a corporation cannot, or will not buy favoritism, they move offshore.

Recently there was a report that because of the resurgence in home building there is a shortage of apprentice carpenters. Government can be blamed for the decline in the housing industry, but that's an article unto itself. According to South Bend School the average wage of an apprentice is about $17,000 annually while other sources have it as high as $31,000 annually. I have found from experience that the type and location of construction can affect wages. A carpenter's helper/apprentice is hard work. Many American youth who have become soft will often choose to go into debt for college rather than seek apprenticeships.

Today we find many of these jobs filled by immigrants, both legal and illegal. This is because many of these people are familiar with hard work and low pay. They also know how to save and to live a frugal life. This is why government looks to pass some type of immigration bill that will provide amnesty for those who came illegally or overstayed visas. In addition, politicians want to give token punishments to those who have failed to pay taxes or have stolen identities.

If we look at most of our economic problems we will find government involvement. Government mandated minimum wages have made young people choose fast food jobs over those in construction that are labor intensive, in harsh weather conditions. The carpenter helper will someday leave the job having learned a skill set, while the fast food worker will walk away smelling like hamburger. Because of government involvement the fast food worker makes the same as the more labor intensive carpenter helper. If we let the free market decide wages then American youth will often choose that job with the highest pay.

Government has a horrible track record at controlling economies. Most of the people elected to office are lawyers and not economists. There are many business people who are elected to office and they use that time to learn how to buy favors. They then go back to the private sector and teach other corporate owners how to play the game. This game must end and the only way that can be done is to take away government's power to play. Those on the left think the game can be controlled by giving the government more power. That's like giving the addict more heroin.

Government Command and Control Farming

Published on
12/26/13 1:27 PM

As Europe clawed its way out from under the ravages of World War 2 the one thing they desperately needed was food.

Farmers had to reclaim farm lands and put them back into production. In an effort to speed the process, European governments began giving financial support to farmers. Their plan worked and they managed to rapidly end hunger.

Seventy years later, and long after formation of the 27 nation European Union, the practice continues. Through subsidies and tight regulation the EU has been able to produce cheap affordable food. Enter 2013 and we find Belgium farmers dumping milk on fields in protest of too low milk prices. Unless something is done many EU farms are threatened by bankruptcy.

By the 90's EU farms were over producing. Reports of wine lakes and mountains of butter – as described by the EU press – made some think it was time to have a more free market approach to agriculture. When the world wide recession hit, and driven unnecessarily deeper by the US government created housing bubble, world food prices dropped dramatically because people were buying less.

Progressive types believe they can control the economy by thinking they know what's best for everyone. Simply because someone is elected to office doesn't make them effective economists. It is only when faced with disaster, such as the one in Europe, will government back away from certain practices. A looming disaster is forcing EU officials to rethink their policies and follow a more free market approach.

A command and control economy has never worked. It was this command and control thinking that created the housing bubble, which resulted in the 2007 recession. Recessions are a normal part of a free market economy. You will always find up and down turns in an economy. Many times attempts to control an economy out of a recession only extends the down turn. The Great Depression is a prime example, as is the 2007 recession.

A command and control economy is based on one thing – a consistent government. Government is always in a state of flux. It is never a single mind. With each change comes a different way of doing things. These changes can be a result of cronyism or simply a lack of knowledge. When you live in a region where everyone has exactly the same government controlled education, thinking will tend to follow a narrow path.

Europe is often amazed by political differences in the USA. They don't understand why so many are constantly talking about politics. The reason is simple, education is a local decision. Each region typically teaches a variety of ethics and pushes the mind in many directions. For good or bad this allows people too look at a single problem from many different perspectives. The more possible solutions the better chance of finding one best suited for that situation.

Each day situations change, especially in economics. The simple trip to work can often require many different decisions each day. Traffic is always in a state of change. The government sets speed limits and lines the roads with signs in an effort to direct traffic flow. A roadway is probably the single thing in the country that has the most government control. Despite that control there are massive traffic jams. You can travel that same route the next day and traffic zooms along normally.

An economy is much the same as a road system. Farm production varies greatly from season to season. The farmer makes many decisions based on weather and what their neighbors grow. Farming is maybe the most unpredictable market supplier. It is usually impossible to predict accurately the annual yield. For something to be tightly controlled results must be fairly predictable. Traffic counters predict road use. Crop history is used to predict outputs. On roadways a traffic jam is typically simply annoying. When agriculture hits a jam it can affect the lives of millions.

We have another variable, and that's the consumer. One season beef can be in vogue and it seems everyone wants red meat. The next year something happens that causes people to become a little more health conscious and they switch to chicken and fish. One year green beans might be in huge demand, while the next it's spinach.

The producers must be free to change direction quickly to supply the variable market. Government is much like an aircraft carrier, it takes a long time for it to change direction – only with government it can take years or even decades for these changes to come. There is no problem when government builds a road on which the economy can travel, but if they clog it with signs and traffic lights it tends to slow. If there is an exit only every 100 miles it can take too long for the economy to correct course.

It's easy to have the European and progressive attitude that everyone has a right to food. Food and water are requirements for sustaining life. People will find food no matter if it's through natural economic action, by theft, or salvaging food discarded by others. It would be wonderful if all food was free – such as a place where rich and poor alike could walk in and take all they want. We know in such a scenario there would be hoarders and those who waste enormous amounts, which would create shortages. It would be impossible for government to predict behavior on that scale.

We could simply have government distribute food according to need. Government is supposedly doing that now with food stamps. How many times have we been in the grocery store to see those with far more food than you could afford and then pay with a government EBT card. In other cases government will allot a family far less than is needed. History shows us that a central government is a poor distributor of goods. If food was to be distributed, it would have to be on a more local level. We also know there is a black market for food stamps. Too often government control creates a black market that often comes with a criminal element. Alcohol and drug prohibitions are great examples.

T. L. Crain

The economics of food, because it's a necessity, is one with which we must give the most trust. Food prices vary according to the local economy and the distance it must travel from point of production to the consumer. This applies to all goods, but with food much of it is perishable and must – at least more desirable – be produced close to the market. Food is also the only commodity that an average American or European can produce themselves. Kitchens all over the world have herb plants within reach. A patio can contain a single tomato plant. In summer it's impossible to predict the number of home vegetable gardens.

Family farms in America are disappearing because of government control and taxes. Each year there is some new regulation that can increase the cost of farming, but controls on production don't allow for these added expenses. Because of federal crop insurance some risk is negated. But this doesn't offset all the other cost of government encroachment onto the farm. This article cannot end without mentioning what's maybe the most destructive force on the family farm, and that's the death tax.

The American Worker

Published on
3/17/14 9:39 AM

The above photo is a common sight after any major storm. Although in this case Santee Cooper is state owned, something of which I am no fan, the distribution is a member owned Cooperative – the workers are with private contractors. In the rural south nonprofit cooperatives are a common phenomena.

The missing photo is one of power line crews working in the Santee, S.C. swamps after a major storm.

Now that's out of the way, let's talk about the photo itself. I might not know the men in that photo, but I personally know many like them. These men and women sometimes left school early, and with determination they managed to get a GED . Some went to a technical college, while others simply started at the very bottom. No matter their start, they work side by side in mountainous regions or low country swamps.

When there is a major outage these men and women find sleep wherever it can be found. They might be found taking an hour nap in one of the trucks, while still wearing their soggy clothing. These are the men and women who make sure your house is cool in the summer and warm in the winter.

You won't find this labor force filled with illegal immigrants. When you see one of them in a mud filled ditch with a pick and shovel, you will find someone who grew up in the region. Their flesh might be a variety of shades, but they are all Americans and South Carolinians.

The point is, you don't have to look south of the border to find people who will do the hard jobs. There are a lot of Americans who will gladly do the dirty jobs. Today we have a school system and too many parents that tell their children they are too good for this type of work. Those same people will look down on those who get dirty for their paychecks.

What these people too often forget is there are many Americans who love getting their hands dirty. There are those who till the soil because they love the work, and not because they will find riches behind the plow.

College is a great thing. Every society needs teachers, scientists, and engineers. Good doctors are in high demand. The problem comes when some of these people are in college simply because they want to earn good wages or have a job where they don't get dirty. This is a huge part of our problems today. We need the best and brightest in college. We want people in college who have earned their way with hard work.

Today's colleges are filled with people who are there simply because they don't want to work. Sometimes the best and brightest are turned away because of state mandated quotas. Sometimes they are forced away because classes are filled with people who would be better suited in a technical or vocational school.

Because government now freely loans money for college, the institutions have increased costs to attend. This happens anytime government becomes involved. In some cases student loans are needed, but those instances are rare. Many people have spent a decade working their way through college. Sometimes along the way they discover a love for their current job, or an opportunity comes their way and they change majors. College is something that should be savored and well thought through.

I have a friend who was working her way though college, as well as receiving a small allotment from the state lottery. She had been working toward an accounting degree when suddenly came the opportunity to buy the business where she worked. Because she had not rushed through college by amassing debt, she was able to change her major to business. She now owns an auto repair shop. Along the way she had to learn through experience pretty much every part on the automobile.

This could happen because her education hadn't been structured by some school councilor that had only the best interest of the institution in mind. Too many people entering college have no idea what they want to do the rest of their lives. It's rare that a child of 18 can know what kind of work they want to do for the next 40 years. Technical college worked out well for me. I enjoyed my work for the next 30 years following graduation, but I know now that work too often didn't fulfill my creative side.

We have the small business owner who many times never graduated from college. They might have attended a few classes needed to operate their business, but a degree was never in the picture. The life of a small business owner is not a bed of roses. You might find him or her one day mopping the floor or unstopping the toilet. You might find them having to break up a fight in their establishment because if he or she sat back and waited for police the damage would be too great to customers and property.

The world takes many different jobs to continue spinning. No job is too large or too small. When the day comes and you feel you are above doing menial tasks, the future will come knocking. For 30 years I earned above average wages. Today I would feel rich with that income. I have since been on jobs that minimum wage would have been a pay raise. I didn't do those jobs for the money, I did them because that's what I wanted. At the end of a long day many self employed people will have worked for wages well below minimum wage.

All jobs and occupations aren't created equal, but the passion with which they are done should be. If you see someone working for a low wage, let that person be content with doing something they love. Don't look down on service workers because you earn your living in a steel tower. If you want to help those around you, vote for those who are best for the economy – those who will not stifle small business with obscene regulations.

Oh yes, the next time you see a line worker sweating in the hot sun or shivering in the freezing cold after a storm, buy them an appropriate drink.

The not so new deal

Published on
9/8/12 1:15 PM

I recently came across this image and text on Facebook. I found the image to be over the top and the accompanying text interesting. I decided to take each bullet point and add my commentary.

Author note: Image was of President Obama's face shopped onto the classic photo of Franklin D. Roosevelt as seen on the cover of Time Magazine. Image removed for possible copyright violations.

Some facts about FDR.

1. Brought the country back from financial collapse.

2. Established and protected Social Security.

3. Worked toward ending a war.

4. FDR was completely opposed to everything Hitler stood for - the biggest threat to national security. Hitler died on April 30, 1945 by taking poison and then shooting himself with a pistol. (corrected)

5. Wife was an advocate of the disadvantaged

6. Invested in jobs and the nation's infrastructure.

7. Spoke to the people not at them.

8. Strong advocate of the military and its soldiers and sailors.

9. Strong foreign policy record in the presence of tyrants.

10. Established and sustained regulation of Wall Street.

11. A champion of minority groups.

12. Ended discrimination in the military.

The Teatarian

Sound familiar?

FDR is consistently considered one of the top three Presidents in history, but the ideological right considers him a dangerous progressive, much the same as with the maligned Obama.

1. Brought the country back from financial collapse.

This is one topic that seems to come up more and more since Obama was elected. There are many comparisons of Obama to FDR. Obama loves to use the comparison himself. I can't talk about this topic without mentioning the fact that some believe segments of the Democratic Party engineered this recession so that they could reclaim the power that Franklin D. Roosevelt and the democrats once held

I am always amazed when people credit FDR for bringing the country back from economic collapse when it was he who kept people in poverty for a decade. Yes, of course what I just said goes against everything you ever heard in school. For a start let's look at the unemployment numbers.

Average rate of unemployment
in 1929: 3.2%
in 1930: 8.9%
in 1931: 16.3%
in 1932: 24.1%
in 1933: 24.9%
in 1934: 21.7%
in 1935: 20.1%
in 1936: 16.9%
in 1937: 14.3%
in 1938: 19.0%
in 1939: 17.2%

We can compare that to the unemployment of today and to that of the previous decade. For almost two decades the country had been at what is considered full employment, which is 4.5% to 5.5%. We can debate the reason for the economic downturn in 2008, but this isn't the time. For now we just know it happened. Since that time we have drifted between 7.9% to 10.1% unemployment. The average tends to linger just above 8%. We are told by Obama this is the new normal. We know it's not normal and never will be.

FDR instituted the New Deal, which in part included the building of infrastructure. We can look around at all the parks and statues to see the things FDR built. Those projects created much needed jobs for which people were grateful. This is why FDR became somewhat of a legend and was elected to four terms. He also installed price controls which froze the price of many goods. This prevented the economy from growing.

Here is the economic lesson we must learn. Price controls can stop an economy decline because it essentially freezes it in place and has a place in the scheme of things. Price controls also prevent the economy from growing. If companies cannot increase profits then they cannot hire additional workers and boost wages.

We can be thankful Obama hasn't taken that route. He does continuously talk about infrastructure spending. The country has an economic cycle that resembles a sine wave. There will be lows and highs. It's during these highs we build infrastructure and send people to the moon. Progressives like Obama and FDR practice Keynesian economics where the government spends during a down turn in the economy. It was this practice in part that helped lock the USA in depression for a decade.

US Gross Domestic Product (current dollars)

The Great Crash, 1929-1933:

in 1929: $103.6 billion
in 1930: $91.2
in 1931: $76.5
in 1932: $58.7
in 1933: $56.4

Obama, for the most part, has been held in check and not allowed to dramatically raise taxes. In his second term FDR also managed growing the economy by not raising taxes. As the economy grows government can spend more because it should be taking in more revenue from the current tax rate. This spending does allow for more economic growth. In 1937 FDR raised taxes and reduced spending which sent the country once more into an economic spiral. This is because so much of the country's economy was based on government spending. The mortal sin in economics is to raise taxes in a recession, even if it's on the rich.

I must reiterate, the so called Bush tax cuts are a decade old and have to be considered the current tax rate. Failing to renew those tax cuts can no way be seen other than a tax increase. This would be an economic sin.

2. Established and protected Social Security

We must first remember that Social Security was in the beginning a volunteer program. The program is run much the same today as it was in the beginning except now participation is mandatory for most people. The big debate today is that Obama and the democrats want to keep it mandatory, while some republicans wish it's return to its voluntary roots where it began.

We also have to look at the budget deficit when looking at Social Security since the trust fund is composed of private Treasury bills. At the time of this writing the Treasury debt is $16 trillion, which makes those t-bills virtually worthless.

Obama has cut the payroll tax which funds Social Security and other benefits. With social Security facing problems, cutting the money going into the fund could have disastrous results later. Instead of saving Social Security he might be hastening its demise. He has turned his head to any attempts at securing Social Security.

In conclusion, we find that Obama differs from FDR in this area.

3. Worked toward ending a war.

This is where there is a huge difference between Obama and FDR. FDR led the country to defeat Japan because we had been attacked. We fought until the enemy was on its knees and destroyed. Japan is now one of our greatest allies.

Obama has essentially surrendered in Afghanistan. He has negotiated to allow the Taliban back into government. We will leave Afghanistan essentially as it was found. I could go into how FDR planned and schemed to get us into a war with Japan and then into the war in Europe, but that can take far too long. I will add some of his words from 1940.

Mr. Roosevelt said at Boston on October 30: "I have said this before, but I shall say it again and again and again: Your boys are not going to be sent into any foreign wars."

The same thought was expressed in a speech at Brooklyn on November 1: "I am fighting to keep our people out of foreign wars. And I will keep on fighting."

The President told his audience at Rochester, New York, on November 2: "Your national government ... is equally a government of peace – a government that intends to retain peace for the American people."

On the same day voters of Buffalo were assured: "Your President says this country is not going to war."

And he declared at Cleveland on November 3: "The first purpose of our foreign policy is to keep our country out of war."

> *4. FDR was completely opposed to everything Hitler stood for - the biggest threat to national security. Hitler died on April 30, 1945 by taking poison and then shooting himself with a pistol. (corrected)*

Hitler worked closely with unions to build his empire. Obama helped orchestrate the handover of General Motors to the unions and the federal government. He did much the same with the Chrysler Corporation.

Hitler, FDR, and Obama have all worked to expand the size and scope of the central government. They all imposed strict regulations on businesses of all types. They were all very business friendly as long as that business toed the party line. Today we see Obama sending copious amounts of money to industries that promotes' his green agenda and donate to his campaign. All three embraced the socialist agenda. The three men may have more in common that this statements portends.

5. Wife was an advocate of the disadvantaged

Who isn't an advocate of the disadvantage? The greatest way to help the disadvantage is to maintain equal liberties for all Americans and to support a healthy economy. Neither FDR or Obama managed to produce a healthy economy while spending trillions on social programs.

6. Invested in jobs and the nation's infrastructure

Obama and FDR invested huge amounts of money in jobs and both have the highest unemployment of any president. It's the private sector that must invest in jobs, not government. Anytime government creates a job it adds little or nothing to the economy. Anytime the government spends/invests money it must first be taken from the economy.

Most of this nation's infrastructure belongs to state and local governments, and often private industry. By increasing taxes the federal government robs these local governments and private industries from growing or doing much needed repairs. The federal government takes money from states and then makes them beg for the money back. When states do manage to get some of that money back it often comes with conditions. I have written often on how the federal government withholds tax money to effect regulations that have already been denied by Congress.

7. Spoke to the people not at them

Both often tell/told people what they wanted to hear.

8. Strong advocate of the military and its soldiers .and sailors

This is an area where FDR and Obama are different. Once FDR committed to military action he supported them morally and financially. Obama and the democrats have time and time again tried to push through spending bills to de-funded military action.

9. Strong foreign policy record in the presence of tyrants.

While Nazi Germany ravaged Europe, FDR did nothing. His speeches supported the isolationist stand of the USA at the time. Obama has apologized countless times to the tyrants of today. He bows before dictators. He refuses to stand with Israel against Iran's development of nuclear weapons. In the Libyan action, Obama said, "We lead from behind." Any general or former president will tell you that one does not lead from the rear.

10. Established and sustained regulation of Wall Street.

This came from both presidents as a result of the financial collapse. It could be said the one good thing FDR did was the safeguard that prevented banks from investing in the stock market. In 1999 Congress enacted, and President Clinton signed into law, the Gramm-Leach-Bliley Act, also known as the Financial Services Modernization Act which repealed parts of the Glass–Steagall Act that prohibited banks from entering the investment, commercial banking, and insurance services since its enactment in 1933. The Glass–Steagall Act was passed in an effort to prevent another chain of bank failures that created the Great Depression. It would have also helped lessen the effects of this recession. Obama's financial reform did not rebuild this wall nor did it cover Fannie Mae and Freddie Mac, the center of the crisis.

11. A champion of minority groups.

For this one let's just look at Obama. Minorities of today have the highest unemployment rate. One can stand on television and talk, but we must look at the results of their actions. The results of Obama's and the democrat's policies have done more to harm minorities. We have to only travel to inner cities and the projects to see the results of the Democratic Party's war on poverty.

When Obama first became president he proudly proclaimed to be against gay marriage. Now that he seeks re-election he has had a change of heart and supports gay marriage. Many of the obstacles for a couple not sanctioned by a government marriage are government induced. As president, Obama and the democrats could have changed the tax laws which would have allowed unmarried couples to file taxes jointly. If he truly cared he would work to change laws that require any marriage to be sanctioned by government.

12. *Ended discrimination in the military.*

I guess this means allowing gays to serve openly. Don't Ask Don't Tell was passed by the Clinton Administration. Having never served in the military I can't best judge what would have been best for the military. I can say the same for Obama; he should have left that decision to those who run the services.

For the past several decades the military has been one of the least discriminating entities in this country.

Reply to a Salon Progressive

Published on
5/3/14 4:15 PM

It's been a long time since I read something that demanded answering in detail. I just read, Piketty shrugged: How the French economist dashed libertarians' Ayn Randian fantasies. The first thing that stood out was that despite referring frequently to Ayn Rand's *Atlas Shrugged*, it's obvious he never read the book. It's also clear he doesn't understand libertarians.

> Parramore wrote:
> *To understand the libertarian view of inequality, let's turn to Milton Friedman, one of America's most famous and influential makers of free market mythology. Friedman decreed that economic policy should focus on freedom, and not equality.*

Right off I have to disregard the fact he called the free market a mythology. Friedman(free market economist) and libertarians believe the focus is on liberty as well as freedom. Also freedom doesn't mean you get to harm your neighbor. The progressive's focus on equality is a waste of time because it's unachievable. No matter how hard government tries it can never make us equal. The best government can do is give us equal opportunity to be the best we can and treat us equally under the law.

> Parramore answered the above mention libertarian concept with this:

> *Basically, the lessons boiled down to this: Some degree of inequality is both unavoidable and desirable in a free market, and income inequality in the U.S. isn't very pronounced, anyway. Libertarians starting with these ideas tend to reject any government intervention meant to decrease inequality, claiming that such plans make people lazy and that they don't work, anyway. Things like progressive income taxes, minimum wage laws and social safety nets make most libertarians very unhappy.*

The thing that makes libertarians unhappy are government programs that wastes money that could be used to help the people about whom progressives seem so worried. The progressive tax they seem to embrace, too often favors the rich. Under the current progressive tax system we find millionaires paying no taxes, or a very low percentage, while poor people still pay into the wasteful system. Their progressive tax system will allow companies like General Electric to come out with a net gain, while people like myself pay. As for problems with minimum wages, I addressed those in, Why Minimum Wage Laws Are Bad.

Welfare can be a good thing, but as I often say, all things in moderation. I have to ask only one question – why work when you don't have to? Permanent welfare removes the incentive to work. I will never forget something from the 60's. Gov. George Wallace's maid had a sister living in Baltimore. The sister told the maid that she should move to Baltimore because there she could make more on welfare than working for the governor – she moved.

Renown economist Milton Friedman said:

"A society that puts equality—in the sense of equality of outcome—ahead of freedom will end up with neither equality nor freedom.... On the other hand, a society that puts freedom first will, as a happy by-product, end up with both greater freedom and greater equality."

To which Parramore replied:

Well, that turns out to be spectacularly, jaw-droppingly, head-scratchingly wrong. The U.S. is now a stunningly unequal society, with wealth piling up at the top so fast that an entire movement, Occupy Wall Street, sprung up to decry it with the catchphrase "We are the 99%."

How did libertarians get it all so backwards? Well, as Piketty points out, people like Milton Friedman were writing at a time when inequality was indeed less pronounced in the U.S. than it had been in previous eras. But they mistook this happy state of affairs as the magic of capitalism. Actually, it wasn't the magic of capitalism that reduced inequality during a brief, halcyon period after the New Deal and WWII.

What Parramore doesn't understand is it's government policies that currently causes money to pool at the top. Because of burdensome regulations and high tax liabilities companies became afraid to invest and expand. In a free flowing economy businesses are continuously expanding and hiring new workers. New businesses are started because others want to get in on the boon. Successful businesses and people all have something in common – they tend to be very competitive. The last thing they want is to sit on their money and become stagnant. They are happiest when expanding and challenging themselves.

The short lived Occupy movement made the 99% become a household term. This is to imply that the 1% wealthy control most of the money and keep it greedily for themselves and it gives the impression of Uncle Scrooge from Donald Duck. The top 1% pay 40% of the taxes, while the top 10% will pay 71% of all taxes. The above statement also implies there is a defined number of dollars., which is simply not true. Because of trade, Quantitative Easing, as well as other means, the amount of US dollars is not constant.

Progressives cling to the Great Depression as their greatest achievement – one of the worst economic times in the history of this country. I am sure the economic gap closed because more people were living in poverty. The gap closed, not because the poor earned more, but everyone's income decreased. Progressives try to claim the economic boon of the 50's as their own – a period when the middle class rose to prominence. Economist like Friedman will tell you that at the end of WWII taxes dropped dramatically. Even the Democratic legend, President John F. Kennedy believed in lowering taxes to allow for the best economy possible. Also because the war had sapped the country of many things people needed to live day to day, this caused an increase in manufacturing, which meant more jobs.

Parramore wrote:
As you'll recall, if you watched the movie Titanic, the U.S. had a class of rentiers (rich people who live off property and investments) in the early part of the 20th century who hailed

from places like Boston, New York and Philadelphia. They were just as nasty and rapacious as their European counterparts, only there weren't quite so many of them and their wealth was not quite as concentrated (the Southern rentiers had been wiped out by the Civil War).

After the Great Depression, inequality decreased in America, as New Deal investment and education programs, government intervention in wages, the rise of unions, and other factors worked to give many more people a chance for success. Inequality reached its lowest ebb between 1950 and 1980. If you were looking at the U.S. during that time, it seemed like a pretty egalitarian place to be (though blacks, Hispanics, and many women would disagree).

Parramore proves himself that appearances can be deceiving. He declares that progressive policies brought about economic equality, while saying a huge segment didn't share in this so-called egalitarianism. I remember while living through government enforced Jim Crow laws how many blacks were delegated to low paid menial task. This was in part because many didn't have the opportunity for even basic education. I'd suggest Parramore stay silent if he can only boast how great things were for white males. By excluding a large segment of the population he can embrace the faux egalitarianism.

He talks about the importance of unions in his so-called egalitarian period. Unions were a great economic boon for the south in the 70's as manufacturers began fleeing to the union free south. Unions and progressive policies have devastated cities like Detroit. In places like Detroit you will find economic inequality at its greatest.

Parramore really showed how little knowledge he had of Atlas Shrugged.

The ironic twist is this: The reason a person like the

fictional John Galt would be able to rise from humble beginnings in the 1950s is because the Gilded Age rentiers lost large chunks of their wealth through the shocks the Great Depression and the deliberate government policies that came in its wake, thus loosening their stranglehold on the economy and society. Galt is able to make his fortune precisely because he lives in a society that isn't dominated by extreme concentrated wealth and dynasties.

In the novel *Atlas Shrugged,* John Galt was an auto worker and had no appreciable wealth. He describes Galt as some rich corporate socialite, when in fact he was the very opposite. He was middle class. While the rich progressive socialites destroyed the economy, he ran away. He moved to the mountains of Colorado where he waited for the world to collapse. It was there that he began building an objective society. Objectivism isn't always the same as libertarianism, but they are very similar.

As if I need further proof that Parramore never read Atlas Shrugged he wrote:

Yet the logical outcome of an economy in which there is no attempt made to limit the size of fortunes and promote greater equality is a place in which the most likely way John Galt can make a fortune is to marry an heiress. So it was in the Gilded Age. So it may be very soon in America.

Galt did become enthralled with Dagny Taggart, CEO of a train company started by her father. She only met Galt after she went in search of him. She wasn't the type to give up and had hopes of convincing Galt to help in saving the country. Anyone who would refer to her as a socialite doesn't know the character. Rand, also wrote in the book how progressive leaders were placing strict limits on corporations. They created the *Fair Share Law* in an effort to equalize incomes and ownership of property.

> Paramore wrote:
> *Actually, there is a very big difference. It is the particular rules governing society that determine who amasses a fortune and what part of that fortune is passed on to heirs. The wrong-headed policies promoted by libertarians and their ilk, who hate any form of tax on the rich, such as inheritance taxes, have ensured that big fortunes in America are getting bigger, and they will play a much more prominent role in the direction of our society and economy if we continue on the present path.*

Progressives believe any wealth amassed during a life time should be given to the government so that it can be divided among the population. Until the left can achieve their progressive Utopia they are content with Death Taxes. These are the same taxes that are driving family farms out of existence because the land is valuable even if the owners live modestly. As I wrote in Warren Buffet and the Death Tax, the super wealthy find ways around progressive estate taxes.

He also portrays libertarians as greedy. Those like him just don't believe people should be able to keep and share with family the things for which they have worked and given their, blood, sweat, and tears. The wealthy are always the largest contributors to charities. They provide jobs so that people can feed and clothe their families.

Ask a progressive to name any country in history that has had a long term existence with progressive governments. Two of these countries come quickly to mind, North Korea and Cuba. Are those the worlds in which you want to live? I'll bet almost no one would trade current day America for either of those countries.

Some might ask why I went to the effort of replying to this man's article. This is one of the best examples I've seen of the progressive mind. There are many like him teaching our children and leading them down the mythical road to a progressive Utopia. Parramore also has the advantage of access to a nationally popular website. His writing will likely reach millions, while mine far less. In this case he holds the position of power and advantage for which he seems to hold such disdain.

Those who think they need an advantage to achieve wealth aren't willing to put in the work to gain that wealth. Sometimes the progressive wealthy like to pretend they are one of the disadvantaged. No matter the case, these people are dangerous because they twist facts to make a lump of coal look like a diamond.

The reason they find it so easy to attract believers in the progressive Utopia is because they see the crony capitalist system of today as the free market. If we have ever had a completely free-market system it was more than 150 years ago. Since the 1800's governments have been trying to manipulate the economic system. I beg people to go learn true economics and then make sure they teach it to their children—You cannot trust schools to teach economic facts.

I know *Atlas Shrugged* is a hard book to read, but again I beg you to read it along with your family. Even if Ayn Rand's Objectivism belief isn't for you, the world in which she wrote is very real. No one is more qualified to write about progressives or communism than someone who has lived in a country where it was the government du jour.

Never forget that the best way to help the poor is with a job and a strong economy. This doesn't mean you can't work with your community leaders to help people who stumble along the way. The farther that help moves away from your community – such as the federal government – the more will be wasted on government bureaucracy.

T. L. Crain

Warren Buffet and the Death Tax

Published on
12/25/10 6:59 PM

Warren Buffet and the Democrats tell us they need to take property from the greedy rich people when they die. The Democrats have decided that you don't deserve any money or property in which you didn't earn. They decided the government has the right to redistribute that wealth

On the surface, all this might sound good to those that believe in wealth redistribution. Once you begin to dig into estate taxes, things may not be what you believed. Warren Buffet pushes hard for the estate tax. There is a good reason he does this, and it's not that he has a kind giving heart. The very wealthy have a way around these estate taxes. They put money into huge insurance policies worth millions. Insurance money isn't taxable through estate or income taxes.

Warren Buffet coincidentally owns many of these insurance companies. As long as there is a death tax he is able to sell these massive policies, which without an estate tax they wouldn't be needed.

There are those who barely fall into the estate tax category, many of which are small farmers. Everyday we hear tales of how family farms are disappearing. The people that own the family farms cannot afford these expensive million dollar insurance policies. When they die, the families are forced to sell the land on which the farms sit. Guess who owns these realtor companies that sell the farms? If you guess Warren Buffet then you are right.

Either way, through sales or insurance, he is reaping billions through the death tax. While he whines that the rich need to pay more in taxes, he starts nonprofit tax shelters in which to hide his money. To be fair, Buffet is giving billions to charity, but if he was really a believer in government redistribution of wealth, then he would turn over those billions to the government.

The left takes our money in the name of doing good. Warren is making millions off deaths of others. We have The Democrats mandating health insurance. Who owns large interest in insurance companies? Yes, Warren Buffet.

I remember the time when people worked and struggled to build a business so their children wouldn't have to do the same. The Democrats have declared the children of these business people don't deserve anything and that if they want wealth they should earn their own.

Welcome to the socialist world of class warfare and wealth redistribution. The government has decided they know better than the men and women that have built the industrial backbone of this nation.

Social Security Trust Fund Theft

Published on
7/24/11 1:19 PM

When the Social Security Act of 1935 was first created by the government, it was a well intended program. When you have politicians involved, even the best intentions often have disastrous consequences. From the beginning social security took monthly contributions/taxes and paid the recipients. By law, any excess revenues must be placed in special-issue, non-marketable Treasury bonds. That is essentially the federal government loaning itself money. The Treasury bonds go into Social Security and the actual money is spent in the general budget.

It is true that by being in the form of bonds, these assets – I use that word loosely – do gain interest, most often 2% or less.

What even the most educated fail to tell you is that this is not truly an asset, but a debt. By turning those excess dollars into treasury bonds, the government could take Social Security funds and spend them any place they wish.

Over decades the Social Security trust has been shuffled around. For the sake of space, time, and understanding, I will reduce the movements to simply these:

1- Social Security was off-budget from 1935-1968;

2- On-budget from 1969-1985;

3- Off-budget from 1986-1990, for all purposes except computing the deficit.

4- Off-budget for all purposes since 1990.

We often find Treasury bills in the account used to show a budget surplus. It's my belief that, in part, it's how Clinton balanced the budget. When counting debt the Clinton, as well as past administrations, counted only publicly held debt. They use an accounting procedure that counts internal debt as assets, even though the government owes itself.

If you checked out the Clinton surplus on factcheck.org you would find it's true, when in fact it's false. I find it impossible to call loaning yourself money an asset. The only place in which to trade those bonds for US dollars is the government itself.

We have heard people say for decades the Social Security trust fund is full of IOUs, which it is, because it's filled with only debt – Treasury bonds. Obama either lied or is ignorant of Social Security when he said, "If the debt ceiling isn't raised, I can't promise those social security checks will go out on the third." Since there are the monthly receipts of Social Security contributions, and other taxes, those payments could easily be made. If the trust fund was as full of money as the Democrats claim, paying recipients wouldn't have even been mentioned. We continuously hear how Social Security is solvent until 2017-2035 – the date is constantly changing. I believe 2017 is the most likely date.

Currently there is enough taxes coming into the Social Security fund to make monthly payments. As baby-boomers continue to retire, eventually those receipts won't cover payments and the Treasury will have to begin buying back those bonds. Unless current debt is resolved, and the economy improved so more tax revenue can be collected, the program will go down in flames on the backs of seniors. Taxing the so-called rich will not solve the problem.

Quantitative Easing and Inflation

Published on
12/20/13 9:29 AM

Recently I was looking at inflation rates and reading what some progressives had to say on economics. I knew inflation rates were low and in part that was due to cheap imports. Imports alone couldn't account for $4 trillion in Quantitative Easing inflation dollars. For the past few days I've been looking for these answers and here are my conclusions.

The answer is far simpler than I imagined, and it also answers a question I had last year. Where are the missing $3 trillion Fed dollars? Today that question would now have to be changed to—Where are the missing $4 trillion fed dollars? The answer is – it's stored at the Federal Reserve in the form of bonds, or at least should be.

The US government has been attempting to practice Keynesian economics. The basic principle of John Keynes economics is that the government pumps money into the economy. That money can come from either borrowing or printing. In the age of computers that money can be created through digital information. It's not important how the Fed created the money for QE. What's important is what happens to all that money.

Right now the Fed is sitting on $4 trillion in bonds accumulated over almost five years of Quantitative Easing. It's hard to determine what the value of those bonds will be at the time they are sold. The eventual problem will be how to inject that money back into the economy without causing hyper inflation. The Fed could simply hand over that money to the US Treasury and be placed into the general fund. The Fed banks could simply keep the money and pay the US government their 6% interest as determined by the Federal Reserve Act.

Now we must look at normal banks. They have been receiving the benefits of all this bond buying and have kept their interest rates slightly lower than they might have been otherwise. Banks have also benefited from the usual borrowing from the fed at less than 1% interest. In a normal reality banks would in turn loan that money to people like you and me, in the form of home mortgages and business loans.

In an iffy economy loaning can be risky. The sub prime mortgage bubble was a lesson learned by banks – not to say the government isn't still pushing banks to give sub prime mortgage loans. The banks find it profitable and less risky to simply invest all that borrowed money back in government bonds and treasuries. The banks are making billions with almost no risk.

The central government has been practicing Keynesian economics from the top down and not the bottom up. To properly inject money into the economy it must be put in the hands of average Americans, not banks. As much as we cringe at hearing the term infrastructure building from the left, it does inject money into the economy by creating jobs done by average Americans. We can debate if infrastructure building is the best way to stimulate the economy another time. What we do know – this isn't what the government has been doing.

We have watched protesters, particularly Occupy Wall Street, fill streets complaining about cronyism. They will debate until they are blue in the face that supply-side economics doesn't work. Yet those same people have been supporting a government that's participating in extreme cronyism by using a mangled form of supply-side. They have created a system in which it's better to hold money than to let it flow into the economy – a system that keeps money in the hands of the rich and powerful.

There is at least $3 trillion dollars kept in offshore corporate accounts. It will remain there as long as the USA has the highest corporate tax in the world. The counter argument to this is that corporations get huge tax breaks. The truth is only the favored get those huge tax breaks and sometimes in the form of cash subsidies. We have a government that has been picking winners and losers through subsidies.

I have just shown $4 trillion plus is held by government, and another $4 trillion dollars held by corporations in American and offshore banks out of fear – both are purposely being kept out of the American economy by government. Progressives constantly talk about the growing divided between rich and poor. They preach to us about cronyism. If there is a divide it's because of a progressive government's economic policies, and not the results of a free market.

We have two possible scenarios. In one, government can release that money all at once back into the economy. This would lead to hyperinflation opening an opportunity for a coup d'Etat. It could be allowed to trickle back into the economy that would give a huge economic boost and allow for an electoral take over. For good or bad this is a dangerous economic practice. We know for sure government does nothing by accident – there's always a plan.

T. L. Crain

Why Minimum Wage Laws Are Bad

Published on
2/14/13 9:42 AM

The right seems to continuously lose the fight against minimum wage laws. It's unpopular to tell people who make low wages they aren't worth more. If a person believes they are worth more they should put forth the determination to prove to an employer they are worthy of that next promotion. When younger, I was one of those minimum wage workers. I was working part time in the summer while school was out. I thought I was rich. I was rich by my standards.

Take the family of four living off the same wage. They would suffer. We must ask where that family would be if there was no minimum wage? It's likely they might have an even lower wage. The worker would have no choice other than seek a job with more pay. That worker, in a healthy economy, will find a job paying more. The previous employer who chose to cut wages, or keep wages low, will likely have to increases wages to fill that job. The market and local economy will always dictate wages for a particular jobs. If you have 1000 potential workers wanting to pick fruit, and jobs available for only 500 people, wages will drop. If there are only 500 people vying for 1000 jobs, wages will increase. The reason wages will go up is that since there are not enough workers, they will try to attract the best workers who will produce more. To attract the best workers employers must pay more.

I remember right after NAFTA passed. I had a friend who often worked south of the border. Because of easy access to the US border, manufacturing began to spring up along that corridor. Those manufacturers were continuously competing for workers because there was not enough people to fill the jobs. Each manufacturer would raise wages to lure workers from a competitor. Workers went back and forth, each time getting an increase in pay.

If government forces the employer to pay a minimum wage, that employer will have several choices. They can pay the wage increase and raise prices on goods and services, or they can reduce the labor force. For a moment let's just stick to the employer who raises prices on services and goods. Those workers are at first happy that they can buy more with their paycheck. As time goes on they find the cost of living has increased because many employers had to increase the prices of goods and services. In a short time the spending power of that larger paycheck is no more than before the wage increase.

This points to why any forced wage increase hurts, or in the end has no prolonged effect, but can be especially harmful if the wage increase is forced on a national level. The USA isn't one huge economy, but thousands of regional economies. It is far cheaper to live in Charlotte, N.C. than New York City. It's for this reason states have their own minimum wage laws.

Another problem with minimum wage laws is they interfere with the free market economy. Anytime government interferes with the economy, there are hiccups. It's hard to say how long these hiccups last, but in time the market will level the playing field. You can be sure there will be jobs loses when wages are increased by force.

The only thing that can help all workers is a strong, stable economy. Wages always go up when there are fewer people vying for jobs. When unemployment is high and people are begging for jobs, employers will lower wages in an effort to hire as many people as possible. Some might argue this isn't fair for the worker. Is it better to pay 5 workers $100 or 10 workers $10? If only 5 are working the other 5 usually have no choice except to live off government. Those 5 receiving income from government produce nothing. If they were working they would be producing, which adds to the economy.

As the economy grows so will, eventually, their wages.

Each year thousands work apprenticeships for no pay. The left says this isn't fair, yet people are willing to work for little or no pay. They do this because it is an investment in the future. They will take what is learned in that apprenticeship and apply it to a future job that pays more than they might have earned otherwise.

Now back to my minimum wage job. If I had chosen to drop out of school and stayed with that employer, and if I put forth effort, I would have worked my way up to possibly being a manager. Destiny was in my hands, not one made by government. The old adage that we must crawl before we can walk can be applied to all aspects of life. Even the low wage fast food worker is learning skills that will pay dividends later in life.

Economic Truths

Published on
12/12/13 9:55 AM

Today we hear a lot about economic and social justice. There seems to always be talk of raising the minimum wage in order to have it keep up with inflation. We hear about the great wealth divide where the gap between wealthy and poor widens. This is spoken as if there is a limited numbers of dollars and if one person gets wealthy they must be taking it from someone at the bottom. This is a fallacy.

Today we have a global market. There is massive trade between countries. Goods and services are exchanged between countries. I could give you the total global accumulated wealth, but that changes daily. The amount of a country's currency changes daily. The USA is creating $84 billion a month. This doesn't include dollars created out of thin air that is loaned to banks. Even if that currency is temporary, it becomes temporarily a part of total currency. Gold and other commodities are converted to cash through Rehypothification in the form of bonds.

Each day wealth is taken and returned to the government. Currently the death tax (estate tax) is 40% of assets above $5.5 million. When the government takes that money it's often returned to the economy in various ways. Eventually that money becomes available to be earned once more. To be sure, this isn't in support of the death tax, but just an explanation of how currency moves. This does show, especially under the current taxing system, the rich cannot accumulate wealth to the point that the poor can have no chance of moving to the middle class.

Death isn't the only way that wealth trickles down to the poor. Much of the wealth lies with business – be it small or large. Most businesses are always looking to expand. They will spend money on building facilities in which to produce more products or services. When expansion happens more workers are hired. Careful thought is given to the number of employees needed. In order to make that decision they must look to see how much of their budget can be set aside for labor. Then they look at the labor market and decide what is the lowest wage that can be offered and attract the necessary skill-set. Skilled labor always comes at a premium, while manually intensive laborers are usually easier to find.

It would be easy to say they can pay these workers a government set minimum wage. This is fine except in some cases that might reduce the number of workers hired. Because of minimum wage laws many manufacturers find it more cost effect to move labor intensive task out of the country. The other option is to bring in illegal workers from another country who are willing to work for a lower wage under the table. Black market wages run in the billions each year. Even though that dollar amount isn't included in government numbers, it is a part of the regional labor market. Many employers will hire $2 an hour labor if it can be found and able to do the job for which they were hired. Even though this is illegal, it happens everyday and is a part of the overall numbers.

The very people who support illegal immigration are the ones crying for minimum wage laws and increases. Economics is like physics, it can't be changed. You can't typically have one thing without giving up another. It's simple to say businesses earn too much. People often forget that many owners of major corporations are are poor to middle class people who depend on income from corporate stocks.

Another aspect of economics is product development. Companies spend millions and sometimes billions on product development. Take large screen televisions for example. When they first came to market $10,000 was the typical price. As wealthy people bought those televisions and the company recouped development costs, prices began to drop dramatically. A product is sometimes out for a decade before they fall into the price range of the average consumer.

When government attempts to control any level of economics there can be unforeseen, disastrous consequences. There are those who sit in their towers of ivory and shout angry rhetoric over economic justice and how you deserve a fair share. The only share that's fair is one for which you have worked. This doesn't mean we need an anarchist free market, but one that is guided by economic sanity. Those shouting the loudest are the ones who seek only their own empowerment and enrichment.

History shows us, and many on the left will admit, that the war on poverty was a failure. Economic justice and fair share is only rhetoric to continue that failed war on poverty. The only thing to have ever produced a large middle class is capitalism. The only thing that can move a person out of poverty, is work. Many have moved to the middle class by selling cast off goods of the rich. There is no impossible barrier keeping someone poor, with health being the exception.

Many of the people trapped in poverty are the mentally ill. Mental illness comes in many forms. Sometimes it's simply the inability to leave the house and interact with others. Those who cry for economic justice would do better to spend their time helping those unable to work, instead of creating division in order to become rich themselves. If people choose to help those who can't work by giving government their money and power, it's best when kept close to home. Your local government better knows what's best for the community than a politician living three thousand miles away.

There is no easy solution. You can rest assured a solution won't come from a bloated central government that's clueless to their own internal happenings. Trust in sound economic principles. There are criminals running businesses and in a free market once they are discovered they lose their customer base. Right now we have government bailing out those criminals when they should have been dissolved or bought by others who are more reputable.

1892 Homestead Strike

While watching the History Channel's *Men Who Built America*, I became intrigued with the Homestead strike of 1892, where 10 men were killed, of which three were Pinkerton agents. History sometimes portrays this as some kind of atrocity. In a sense it was, but who was really at fault? We could blame Carnegie Steel's Fricke, but that is too easy.

Working conditions were hard, but that was life in America in those days. Those people worked twelve hours a day in torturous heat. Those men were steel workers who were known for their toughness.

In comes the union who told the men they needed more

money, which was fair. The unions took things too far. They convinced those workers the steel mill belonged to them and they were the ones who built the business. Unions and the left are telling people the same things today. They tell people that those who built the industry couldn't have done it without the workers, which is true in some sense. It's this kind of thinking that leads many of us to say that unions and the Democratic Party are communistic. They overlook the fact they were given much needed jobs in which to feed their families.

Carnegie Steel agreed to give workers a 30% raise, which is beyond fair, only the union wanted 60%. The strike began and workers barricaded themselves inside the steel mill. Frick found people willing to work, mostly immigrants. Those immigrants were glad to work for the lower wages. We see the same thing happening today. There is a flood of immigrants crossing the southern border to take jobs at lower wages.

Fricke hired the Pinkerton Detective Agency to tear down the barricade and remove striking workers so the steel mill could return to operation. It must also noted that across the country building projects were in danger of stoppage due to a lack of steel. In the end, a lot of people could be harmed other than those huddled behind union barricades.

Ten men died and many others were injured that day, all because greedy union bosses brainwashed those men into believing they owned something they didn't. The steel mill was soon back in operation with replacement workers. In the end, those men died for nothing.

I also see this as a demonstration of union power – even in those early years. A group of men took over a facility owned by an American citizen and police officials did nothing to recoup that property for owners.

Too often we find government and the media choosing sides. When they decide some entity is the bad guy, such as Wall Street and banks, anything done against them is justified. The left demonizes banks, while handing them billions of free money. Imagine if someone would give you a million dollars to use for a week. Imagine the thousands you could earn from simple interest alone.

The Occupy movement took parks hostage while screaming about evil banks and Wall Street, all the while living off union funding. Unions filled crowds with people that directed emotions in directions that worked best for the organization. They used the crowds to push the Democratic Party as the party of choice, while at the same time that party was feeding money to the very people about whom they protested.

Unions collect dues, sometimes forced by law, to send billions to the Democratic Party. In a sense they own a political party that gives it more and more power. Yes, today unions are a dying breed, but that's only because their policies have forced industry after industry out of the country or into southern states where unions are rare.

Unions sent those steel workers to die for their own greed. A 60% wage increase would have been a huge increase in union dues. The left shouts that people have a right to work, while they care nothing about those who invest large amounts of time and money to build facilities in which these people can earn a living. I should maintain the right to decide who does or doesn't work for me. That right should remain with those who risk everything to provide jobs.

I find it odd that the very people who preach workers rights also support illegal immigration. Those on the left should know that labor is a commodity and its worth is controlled by supply and demand. If there is a field where qualified workers are rare, wages soar. If it's an area where workers are plentiful, then wages drop. Unions attempt to defy the market and this rarely ends well. That employer will eventually move to where there is a fair market.

T. L. Crain

Communism falls and Thanksgiving Rises

Published on
2/28/12 11:26 AM

United States history holds one of the best examples ever of communism's failure. We all have heard the fanciful tale of how Thanksgiving began. We have all heard how the poor ignorant Europeans settled in Virginia and didn't know how to grow crops to feed themselves. I clearly understand how varieties in land can make farming hard, and sometimes nearly impossible.

Europeans had roamed several continents, all the while managing to feed themselves. It was only when they came to some of the most fertile soil on the planet that they began to starve. We are told that if not for the indigenous population settlers would have perished.

Something did happen in Virginia. Those people were starving and then suddenly their fields flourished. That transformation was in government, not all in agriculture. In the beginning they were a collective society, Communist, if you must say the word. During harvest all crops were brought to central storage where the village elders made sure each household received their fair share. How many times have we heard that term from Obama and other socialist?

There were people in the village who worked harder than others. Some realized, consciously or subconsciously, that they could produce less and still have as much food for their family as did other villagers. Like some plague this sloughing spread its way thought the village until they were near starving.

At some point the village was forced into a free-market society. Hard working people became tired of providing for the slackers. People began to provide for themselves. Neighbors traded their surpluses with neighbors. Slackers saw the hard workers always had their root cellars full, and their children always wore the better clothes. This encouraged them to double the size of their own fields so they would have extra crops to trade for new clothes. In time the village's best seamstress no longer had to toil in the fields for food. She would sew all day while people traded their crops for the clothes she made.

This is how all societies must work, or they fail. In those days if someone's house burned to the ground, they gathered together and and worked until that house was rebuilt. Now we probably don't have many neighbors that would know how to build a house, so we pay insurance companies for that same service.

In today's government controlled country, neighbors would find it impossible to build that house. First of all, trees could not be milled from their own property and used as lumber because they wouldn't have the proper government stamp. The neighbors couldn't work on the house because they haven't had the proper government training in construction and safety.

Unless the family who lost their home has the proper liability insurance, they wouldn't dare let the neighbors onto their property. If one of those neighbor's slipped and fell they would likely take the people's property in damages.

Has this country gone full circle to the point where our future is the same as history, and we are going to starve like those first settlers? The only way a communist society can exist is if the sloths are banished.

T. L. Crain

Morality

Marriage – Until Death Do Us Part

Published on
4/5/14 6:57 PM

The argument over gay/same-sex marriage rages on to the point people are losing their jobs – as in the case of Mozilla CEO, Brendan Eich who was forced to resign for his contributions to Prop 8 in California(essentially banning gay marriage). In every war there are civilian casualties – in this one the greatest casualty might be that of speech and those who love one another. This battle has put family members at odds with one another.

Let's talk a little about marriage itself. For the first half of this country's history people simply went to their priest or priestess, depending on the religion, for their marriage or hand-fasting. In some cases couples simply cohabited. These unions were often recorded in the family bible, along with the names of future children. When government began keeping records, this is where they went for information.

After the slaves were freed, and sometimes before in free areas, government began to notice that black and white couples were getting married. There were those who thought this joining might tarnish white purity. For that reason they began passing laws to forbid these unions. It was for this reason government decided to take over marriages from religious organizations. There were instances where government forbade those of different faiths to marry.

Today a marriage performed by a government bureaucrat,

or one by a priest or priestess, are equally legal. The government decides who can or can't take part in these government sanctioned marriages. They decide who can take part in the privileges set aside for those married couples. Justice Kennedy noted 1100 statues that pertain only to married people.

A marriage was intended to be something much more personal than a set of government privileges. A marriage is suppose to be about the communing of two lives. It is about two people falling in love and joining for the rest of their lives. Marriage is not about the potential for children, but two people who wish to show a commitment to one another. A marriage is the promise of life together. Many children are produced outside of marriage.

I once participated in one of those government sanctioned marriages and from the day of "I do" until the day of "I'm done" only eleven months had passed. It cost a whopping 250 dollars in 1975 to a lawyer and government to end that marriage. I vowed that day to never again participate in a government sanctioned marriage.

My next long term relationship, not sanctioned by government, was for "Until death do us part." You know you are committed when you hold their hand while vomiting after Chemo. You know you are married when the person to whom you have committed awakens one day and doesn't know your name. You know you have committed to marriage when you raise that person's adopted child as your own. You know you were married when you sit holding the hand of that child at the funeral. I needed no government to tell me that I was married – I needed no government paper to know that I had committed "Until death do us part."

It's time all Americans are treated equally and end government sanctioned marriages. The couple who cohabits should enjoy the same rights as those who stood before some government bureaucrat offering meaningless words. We have contractual law that can cover all possibilities that is now covered by marriage laws. Marriage and being responsible for children aren't the same thing. Taking care of the life you created is a personal responsibility, and those who fail to provide that should be punished. Marriage has never, and never will, make good parents, especially one sanctioned by some oppressive government that decides who can or cannot commit under the same legal rights as their neighbor.

By demanding laws be changed to allow gay marriage you are simply calling for an expansion of government power. The demand should be to get government out of marriage. A marriage should be two people in love standing before family and friends making a life long commitment, not some stranger because you need government privileges.

No matter if you are Christian, Atheist, or Pagan, you should reserve marriage for your own beliefs, and not those of government. Marriage is much more personal than a government certificate. When the person to whom you have committed sits before you bald and ill from Chemo, no government paper will make life better. In some instances it can even make it worse. The next time you find someone to whom you want to commit, forget government and make it personal – "Until Death Do US Part."

Social Conservatism vs Bigotry

Published on
2/5/13 10:01 AM

This country is built on the foundation of freedom to worship as we please. The founders remembered a time in Europe where kings allowed only one religion. Because government and church were so intertwined great minds like Copernicus were executed as a heretic for simply believing the

Earth wasn't the center of the universe. Our founders wanted to insure the same thing never came to pass in the new country.

Despite that dream this country has struggled to keep government and church separated, while all the courts have maintain that separation. Alcohol prohibition was one of the most violent periods in modern times. This prohibition was based on religious beliefs. Eventually the folly of the 18th Amendment was overturned. Today the country faces the same problems with the declared war on drugs. This country learned nothing from its previous mistake. No matter the political party in power, the war on drugs continues. I dare say the war on poverty has had the same disastrous effects.

This isn't about drugs or alcohol. This is about that same power being used to control segments of the population. Over the course of history there have been many laws created to control people by race, religion, or gender. FDR has been proclaimed one of the greatest presidents ever, yet he detained thousands of Japanese Americans in interment camps. There are few people alive today that look back on that imprisonment with anything other than disdain.

In November of 2012 we watched as the Democratic presidential candidate won re-election by a landslide despite a suffering economy and 8% unemployment. Their entire campaign was based on a social agenda. The war on women was false, but they made enough believe it to be factual. They used the bigotry of social conservatives to their advantage.

Today the great social war centers around homosexuality. I have written time and time again how the gay marriage problem would go away if government removed itself from the equation. There is no need for government to remain involved in marriage. If the government simply taxed all people equally, contractual law can handle any potential problems. Despite the democrats' supposed stance in support of gay marriage, even they refuse to remove government from the equation.

It's been said that the only way the Republican Party can continue to exist is if they separate themselves from the Conservative movement. This battle has been going on for a very long time. I should make it clear that it's the social conservatives about which they speak. There are those social conservatives who fight vehemently against gay marriage. In some respect they have a legitimate argument. They believe the term marriage relates to their religious beliefs. I believe to some extent they have a valid argument.

The problem lies in how some argue. As someone who has read many of the Tea Party websites I have seen posters who can be described no less as bigots. I have seen some call for the death or incarceration of anyone who is gay. Because the site managers do not moderate this hate speech, they are seen as supporters. I know of one Tea Party site from which I was banned for defending the right of gays to exist, not just marry. The GOP will distance itself from these groups. This is also what has done, maybe unrepairable, harm to the Tea Party brand.

The most recent issue comes from the possibility of the Boy Scouts of America admitting gay youths. We will hear the homophobes screaming how Obama has gotten to the BSoA. The president recently spoke out in the matter, offering his support for the admittance of gays. This is not a matter for government. The BSoA is a Christian based organization and can choose to do what it pleases. I personally believe that their desire to leave the possible decision to local groups is the correct one.

Social conservatives are against homosexuality because they see it as a sin, or an abomination to God. In a free country people have the right to these beliefs. What they don't have a right to is forcing these beliefs onto others. The US Constitution is adamant that all people are equal under the law. We cannot impose different laws for any one segment of the population if we are to be a free country and uphold the

Constitution as the foundation of our laws.

I have come to the conclusion that we do need a third party in this country. The social conservatives should go their own way. Many have shown they can't work with those with different beliefs. If this happens we might can salvage the Tea Party brand and work to make the GOP the party of the Constitution. There are those like myself who have tried to work along side bigots in an effort to save this country from bankruptcy. This unholy alliance has become harder with each passing day.

There is nothing wrong with the belief that a traditional marriage might be best for raising children. We do know that the broken family is a huge problem and causes many of today's ills. This also doesn't mean that a gay couple can't offer the same stability as heterosexuals. We will find bad parents in every gender and sexuality.

I typically avoid the abortion issue because it always brings with it extreme emotions. This is one area where I do understand the social conservatives. They are defending life. I personally find late term abortion criminal unless there are extraordinary circumstances. I also believe government should never pay for abortion unless there are extraordinary circumstances. It is wrong to take tax dollars from Americans and spend it on a procedure that brings about such strong feelings of disagreement.

No person is going to agree 100% on any political agenda except their own. What we should agree on is taking these decisions out of Washington and placing them in the hands of individual states. People from South Carolina are as different as the moon and sun from those in California. For those who put their social agenda first and want a larger and more powerful federal government to advance their religious beliefs, it's time for you to form your own party. The Republican Party has never been for a stronger central government no matter the issue. We do not want a federal government deciding what is and isn't moral.

Those of us considered the political right should at least agree that we need to limit federal power. We can then battle each other on the local level when it comes to social issues. Unless some of you can contain your bigotry and work with groups like Log Cabin Republicans or GOProud, then we don't need you. It's time for you to go form your new party. To defeat socialism and communism we need only those who want a smaller, less powerful, central government in all areas.

Equality For All (Revised)

Published on
8/24/11 1:00 PM

This is a revised version of a piece I wrote in November of 2010.

Let's begin with that the fact that no group is for equality for everyone. If we look deep within ourselves we will find prejudices, or just unknowingly create inequalities. Progressives are always talking about taxing the rich to help pay for those less fortunate. If everyone is truly equal, how can you make one person pay more in taxes than another? The answer is simple—you can't.

The left will ask, "How do you help the poor if you don't tax the rich?" You help them by getting out of their life. I was talking with a gentleman in South Africa and he mentioned Shanty Town. This is an area that is government owned land where the poor began to build small shanty homes in which to live.

This made me think about how in America the Federal government is making gigantic land grabs, while at the same time taxing the so-called rich, supposedly in an effort to help the poor. I watched as local governments began to ban or greatly restrict mobile homes because they provided fewer property taxes. These are homes that the less fortunate can easily afford.

Our government decided they didn't want people living in shanty towns or mobile homes, so they came up with the Community Reinvestment Act and began to throw around terms such as affordable housing. The federal government used its might to force banks to give home mortgages to people who could barely afford them. When the economy declined and interest rates dropped these people began to refinance their homes with the lower variable rate. In time those rates began to rise, so much that these people lost, or will lose, their homes. In some cases monthly payments doubled.

If the same people had lived in a cheaper mobile home, or some cheaper home of their own design, then the collapse of the US economy might have never happened. If people were truly free to live their lives, economy down turns would be more local than national.

Every state and community has building codes for all structures. The government does this, they claim, for our own protection. They use the excuse that you should build a house to certain specifications so that it won't lose its resale value. They tell us they want to make sure the house is safe in which to live. Those are all lies.

The truth is, they also don't want to live next to a shack, which would hurt the value of their home. In rural America many homes are hidden deep inside forests where no one can ever see them, yet they are forced to build by the same codes. If one builds a house in which they never plan to sell, and is out of view, why should the government care about the house's looks?

We don't need government to make sure houses in our neighborhoods meet a certain standard. There are home associations which do that quite well. It's clear government wants homes to be as expensive as possible so that it can collect as much tax as possible. We must get government out of our private lives. The poor can never truly have affordable housing as long as government intrudes. There are also insurance companies that can determine the quality of a home since they have a stake in the structure.

Until the late 1800's a couple didn't need a government license to get married. People that wanted to spend the rest of their life together, either just moved in together, or they went to their place of worship where through a ceremony that was sanctioned by the church, became married. The church performed any divorce.

Today we have the gay marriage argument. We are having this debate only because government became involved in the marriage business. We don't need government telling us with whom we can spend the rest of our lives.

Someone asked me when I brought up this argument, "Unless a gay lover is married they can't see their partner in the hospital." I answered with: "The hospital is a private business and has nothing to do with government. In this case it's the hospital that should be picketed, and not the local congressperson." Get government out of marriage and the gay marriage debate vanishes. The only reason government became involved in marriage to begin with was to prevent blacks and whites from marrying.

Since originally writing the above paragraph I have been reminded of the privacy laws enacted by Clinton. I won't say that we didn't need some privacy regulation, but as always government takes things too far. Thanks to these laws a health-care professional can no longer tell the mother of an unconscious 18 year old child any details of the illness or injury. Thanks to this government over protection we must now have consent forms with our children and other family members. These same consent forms would be needed with any partnership if government removed itself from marriage.

If everyone is taxed individually, and as equals, a lot of

problems are solved. Over the years people have been taxed at either higher or lower rates just because they chose to be married. We give tax breaks to people that choose to have children. Many of these different tax breaks came about because politicians used them to gain favor with voters. Why do we want to give tax incentives for child birth? Do we not already have a population problem?

Anyone who chooses some religious, or personal ceremony, the joining would be legally bound and structured with contracts. These contracts can be of your own choosing. If and when the couple decides to terminate their relationship, these contracts would be the basis for any settlements. Government could even set minimum standards for these contracts, which it does already. Churches could set their own standards for divorce, which some do today.

Never let those on the left tell you they are the ones for freedoms, because in a sense they take more than they ever give. The only thing the left knows is to give out special rights to different groups of people. They fight for rights from bullies, hate speech laws, hate crime laws, rights for people with different skin colors, and gay rights. Anytime we bestow special rights on someone, the rights of another are lessened. We already have laws that protects all people equally. What we need is equality for all and equal application of laws.

Boy Scouts Admit Gays

Published on
5/24/13 11:38 AM

The Boy Scouts of America has made the decision to allow openly gay scouts. Since the beginning, scouts have had sexually active gay boys in the organization. Allowing the boys who are openly gay to join the scouts is the correct thing. I think It would be better to know which boys were gay so that on outings they aren't allowed to share tents and cabins. This would be essentially the same as separating sleeping arrangements by gender.

People running the scouts currently will not allow gay leaders. For some reason too many people believe gay adults are pedophiles, while statistics show otherwise. The anti-gay people point to a 1988 study (**Erickson et al. (1988).** *Behavior patterns of child molesters.* **Archives of Sexual Behavior, 17, 77-86**) that says 86% of the men found molesting boys were gay or bisexual. I dare to argue that a straight male won't molest young boys, but they will molest young girls. We can apply the same statistic that 86% of the molesters of young girls are male. All stats bare out the fact that the majority of child molestation comes from males. If we apply the logic that 86% of child molestation comes from men, then maybe the scouts should allow only female scoutmasters.

We can look to any conservative, and many republican websites to find disdain at the decision of the scouts to allow openly gay boys. Most often that disdain will be followed by a quote from the bible. At some point the writers will point out that they have many gay friends, but that they find the act sinful and that it's an abomination to God. I personally ask, how can anyone be friends with someone who views them in such light?

I have written many times how the left uses the topic of homosexuality against republicans. All they have to do is mention the word "gay" and any discussion board will fill up with how God hates gays. If a political party is to succeed they must treat all people as Americans, with all having the same rights under the law. When a party uses the bible to give liberty to some while denying it to others, it will soon fail.

For decades the bible has served republicans and conservatives well. Both parties have made laws based on religion. The democrats used the bible to support slavery and segregation. Times have changed since the 50's Even though most people still identify with being Christian, they are more open to social change. Even many gay people are Christian. We find ourselves living in a time where sex out of marriage is common and generally accepted. We are finding sodomy and laws pertaining to consenting sex disappearing from law books.

If republicans and conservatives continue with speech that can be taken in no way other than bigoted, the party will go the way of dinosaurs. For me, that would be sad because they are the only political group that has so many other things right. Social conservatives will be the tool used to propel communism and Marxism into the mainstream. Many people will run from social conservatives. When someone runs away, they will eventually run into something. The left gives some convincing arguments on how their policies can work. When personal acceptance is backed by the promise of a Utopian society, they will stop running and cling to that new friend.

With the IRS targeting conservative and Tea Party organizations some on the left support the IRS. The reason being they view those groups as racist and bigoted. This country has become more divided than ever. The left and right too often have strong hate for the other. I see both democrats and republicans embracing tyranny as long as it's their own.

This is a fight where both parties cannot survive. Only one will come out as the dominant majority and that will be the Democratic Party. Right now, as always, the democrats are over reaching and that might weaken them for a while, but in the end they will win. I think that no matter which party becomes dominant or they both go back and forth, America will be the loser because no matter the party, government grows bigger and more domineering.

T. L. Crain

Progressive – not gay agenda

Published on
4/4/14 10:43 AM

Occasionally something comes along that I find completely astounding and outrageous. I will begin this to say that I am a happy Mozilla user, not because of their politics or any other reason – I simply finds their products fulfill my needs.

Mozilla's chief executive officer Brendan Eich, was let go this week because in 2008 he donated $1000 to Proposition 8 that sought to make traditional marriage the standard in California. The proposition gained popular vote and passed, that is, until struck down by courts. Right or wrong the system went through the process.

The problem comes when an American donated to a particular cause in which he believed and then 6 years later forced from his job for that donation. I personally don't agree with his political choice on this matter, but I will defend his right to disagree with my opinion. In my perfect world government would not have any say on whom married or didn't marry. We know from past experience with interracial couples that government has had poor judgment in this area.

The problem in this instance is that a small group of individuals forced a company to fire a man for voicing his political opinion – not by standing on a podium making proclamations, but by quietly making a donation. I am guessing those calling for his dismissal will not be aware of the firestorm they have created.

There are many who will blame this on the gay agenda. Let me say now there is no gay agenda, only a progressive agenda that operates in the name of homosexuals. There are gay Republican groups like Log Cabin and GOProud where some are for gay marriage, but would decry the destruction of free speech. There are many gays who simply avoid politics, but would love to enjoy the same rights, legally and spiritually, as heterosexual couples. Many of those same people would be saddened that some small group of individuals has cost a man his job, not for bigoted hiring practices, of which there is no evidence, but for simply practicing his 1st Amendment right to speak out against government or to partake in the government process.

The progressive, not the gay, agenda is to squelch all speech by those who think differently. They will stop that speech through mockery, and even worse, by using race or by portraying that speech as hate. They will proclaim to operate in the name of minority groups. We see today that whether it be women or minority rights groups, they protect only progressives within that spectrum. This is the difference between libertarians and progressives—The libertarian will especially protect the speech with which they disagree. Popular speech rarely needs protection, but it is the speech of the few – those who think differently – that most needs our protection.

I am disappointed that Mozilla succumbed to those who wish to squelch speech and the free exercise of the political process. Even though I do not agree with Brendan Eich's position, I will protect his right to that choice. Once we live in a country where people are afraid to speak opposition to the majority or those with the podium, then we have taken the road to ruination. At one time people were afraid to speak out publicly against slavery. Had people been allowed to speak freely, slavery might have never existed in this country.

To those who use all gays to promote your political agenda, tread carefully. There are many bigots and potential bigots in the country and you are only feeding that bigotry. Those who lead the so-called gay agenda have done more harm to gays than good. To win political ground you must convince people that your side is correct. By using coercion you force many to run away. The wild animal will run if you chase it screaming. If you approach that animal with treats and understanding then that animal is more likely to follow you home.

For once do the honorable thing and stop letting a few progressives lead you down the path of fanaticism. Offer Brendan Eich an open hand and try to convince him why he is wrong, just as I will try to convince you, the progressive, that government controlled marriage is the wrong path. In order to prevent government from making this mistake in the future you must now take the power of marriage out of their hands. When all Americans are treated equally by government then we truly live in a free country.

I should add, this is one of the main dangers of having to disclose donations. It is for exactly this type of retribution that we must change political donation laws to keep them private. We cannot let public pressure ban opposing speech.

Duck Phil Platypus

Published on
12/21/13 9:31 AM

Duck Phil Platypus is the perfect title for this article because the Phil Robertson story is one of the ugliest I have seen in a very long time. I'm not sure if by the time this fades into the twilight of news that anyone will have been correct. For the most part, this is much ado about nothing. But since it has become something there is a lot that needs to be said.

Let's start by quoting some of his comments:

Phil On Growing Up in Pre-Civil-Rights-Era Louisiana

"I never, with my eyes, saw the mistreatment of any black person. Not once. Where we lived was all farmers. The blacks worked for the farmers. I hoed cotton with them. I'm with the blacks, because we're white trash. We're going

across the field.... They're singing and happy. I never heard one of them, one black person, say, 'I tell you what: These doggone white people'—not a word!... Pre-entitlement, pre-welfare, you say: Were they happy? They were godly; they were happy; no one was singing the blues."

Phil is referring to the days of share croppers and blacks lived on the farms where they worked. Farms varied greatly, as did the houses in which the black workers lived. Some houses were relatively nice, while some were no more than roughly built shacks. This sounds to also be during the days of Jim Crow laws. Were southern blacks happy? Likely for the most part, but we must ask – were they equal? Not even close.

Was the life of a share cropper easy? Life was harsh for the share cropper no matter if you were black or white. But people worked hard and managed to survive. A few sharecroppers even managed to make enough to eventually buy their own land. Some used the success to created a business outside farming. Life in the 50's rural south was rarely easy. No matter if a person was black or white it took hard work to survive.

Phil and I are near the same age. I was a senior in school as I watched blacks ripped from their own school and forced into a too small school with a bunch of white people who were just as disgruntled. I watched as blacks and whites attacked one another with fists and clubs. I truly didn't see a lot of happy black people. I saw people who had been forced by a political system to give up their long held traditions in a misguided effort of forced equality. As a teenager I was completely confused by the things I saw. Despite being raised by a racist and bigoted father, I had a mother who was raised in poverty and taught me to judge people as individuals.

This was a period during the Vietnam war – a war that few people understood. Most, black and white, only knew that their sons were leaving home and never coming back. The late 60's and early 70's were virulent times. Those were times of change.

This was also the dawn of the welfare state. The results are still in the making – so far it's not a pretty picture.

I had intended to write this about Phil's gay comments since they seemed to be the ones that caused the most drama, but I found the ones about blacks more thought provoking. Let's begin by quoting the comments of most interest.

> *"It seems like, to me, a vagina—as a man—would be more desirable than a man's anus. That's just me. I'm just thinking: There's more there! She's got more to offer. I mean, come on, dudes! You know what I'm saying? But hey, sin: It's not logical, my man. It's just not logical."*
> *"Everything is blurred on what's right and what's wrong,"* he says. *"Sin becomes fine."*
>
> *GQ: What, in your mind, is sinful?*
>
> *"Start with homosexual behavior and just morph out from there. Bestiality, sleeping around with this woman and that woman and that woman and those men,"* he says. Then he paraphrases Corinthians: *"Don't be deceived. Neither the adulterers, the idolaters, the male prostitutes, the homosexual offenders, the greedy, the drunkards, the slanderers, the swindlers—they won't inherit the kingdom of God. Don't deceive yourself. It's not right."*

These are words you'll hear from almost any Christian. Pretty much everything is a sin it seems, but those are usually at the top of the list. Phil is who he is and will continue to be that person – like him or not. I dare say someone from a northern city might have said the same thing and no one would have cared. There is a certain discrimination for southerners when it comes to speech. We know that from the Paula Deen incident where she was fired for a twenty year old comment. It has become clear people aren't treated equally for their speech.

The Teatarian

A&E had a decision to make. I can only guess what might have been behind their decision. It could have been because one of the top executives has a gay child, or might be gay themselves and took offense at being called a sinner. It could have been as simple as a company knowing it's demographics. Even though Duck Dynasty has great ratings, it is only one show of a large and popular network. Time will be the gauge as to if A&E's decision was the correct one for them.

There is a reason the gay community is sensitive to remarks like Phil's. Gay youths and adults have suffered everything from abusive language to mortal beatings simply because they were born differently. Even if some choose to believe being gay isn't something that is a result of birth, they often belief it's a mental illness. In either case gays are Americans.

This is a free country and people are free to say and be who they please. There are often consequences for speech or simply being yourself. You can say things in peer groups that can't be openly said. People have been punched or beaten for practicing their free speech. The same has happened to people who by chance of birth were born in the wrong town and are openly gay.

The 1st Amendment only guarantees that government can't limit your speech, but as we all know if you call your neighbor an SOB there are likely to be consequences. This is why we often guard our speech as to anger as few people as possible. Phil stated his belief and we all as Americans should offer him support. GLAAD(*Gay & Lesbian Alliance Against Defamation*) and A&E also stated their beliefs, which should also be respected. Respecting speech doesn't mean you must agree.

I should add that GLAAD doesn't and cannot speak for all gays. I see their actions as a disservice to the gay community. There are a lot of people who will blame all gays for what they say and do. This is for the same reason all Christians or Baptists shouldn't be blamed for the actions of Westboro Baptist.

This entire episode in the scheme of things has been blown completely out of proportion. The country is facing economic collapse. We have a government that refused to give a cost of living increase to veterans who fought for this country. Yet the biggest topic is of some millionaire family that might have to move their show to a different network, or discontinue it all together. If people want to watch families like the Robertson's, move to the rural south – they are likely to be your neighbors.

When Church and State Collide

Published on
9/4/13 2:51 AM

There has been a major debate over a small time bakery and other businesses that refused service – based on religious belief – to gay couples preparing for marriage. In some cases suits were filed and won by the gay couples. This is not about the cases themselves, but the dangers that lie ahead.

Let's begin by my stating that I do believe a business has the right to refuse service for many reasons. I think businesses that don't want to serve gays should put up a sign to indicate their desire. This would give gays and their supporters notice to not spend money with these businesses. The greatest part of being American is the right to make choices, especially informed choices.

We often wonder from what vantage point a person writes, so I want to state that I personally don't believe government should be involved in marriage because all Americans should be equal under the law. Because government chose to interject itself in personal relationships, a dangerous door was opened.

Conservative Christians are quick to tell us that marriage is between a man and a woman, as well as a rite belonging to the Christian doctrine. Let's for a moment assume they are correct

126

and marriage is property of the Christian church.

Those service businesses in question have chosen to base their decision of not serving on religion. The gay couples wanting to be married are doing so because without marriage they cannot enjoy certain liberties. A judge has said that marriage affects 1100 different laws and regulations. One of the most discussed aspects are taxes and inheritance. If there were no advantages to filing a joint tax return, there would be no need for that aspect of the tax code. No matter if the couple is of the same sex or traditional, they seek marriage for the same reasons, it makes legal sense.

If marriage belongs to the Christian religion, could it not be said that the church uses government to force a Christian practice on non Christians? Those businesses that refused service and their supporters are angry that government is forcing them to participate in a function with which they disagree on religious grounds.

Let's turn this around and look at the many things forced on non Christians. There are holidays such as Christmas and Easter that are Christian. Even though Easter isn't on the list of federal holidays, federal workers are dismissed on a designated day to give them an extended weekend. In essence, federal workers are required to participate in Christian holidays no matter their personal belief.

When Americans are elected to office or become an officer in the military they are required to give an oath in the name of God. We find the Ten Commandments on the wall of the Supreme Court. We find religion mixed with government in too many places to mention.

Because Christianity is already a part of government, the church has given a part of itself to government. Because of this marriage between religion and State, one can't be surprised when government begins directing when and where personal religious beliefs cannot be applied.

When the church applies for a tax exemption, they know

that exemption comes with strings. There are certain things the church can't do once they accept the exemption, such as limitations on political activities. Once government began making laws that favored citizens who are married, it then claimed the power to insure those favoritism are applied equally to all.

Too often the line between government and religion is blurred. Government locates election polls in churches and other buildings belonging to the church. When asked to testify in a court of law a bible is offered on which you must place your hand – there are alternatives. But the fact that it is offered in a government proceeding should be worrisome to the Christian church. Christians might wake someday to find rites from other religions forced on them. Until the church separates itself from government, it can't be surprised when government tells people when and where they can practice their faith.

Blogging – The new bully?

Published on
5/10/14 11:54 AM

I have been wanting to write about the Benham brothers, but facts seem to be elusive. I was also at odds as to what approach to take. As of today it's only the brothers speaking. So far HGTV has been silent on the matter. It is for this reason I have only the brother's words on which to base my writing. Now to start at the beginning.

This week it came to light that two brothers were suppose to have a house flipping show on HGTV. The show never aired because of statements made by the brothers. As with Phil Robertson, it came down to their comments about homosexuals. Even though they try to make it about traditional marriage, it's much more. David and Jason Benham have often quoted bible verses as they crusaded against same sex marriage. For this reason they have been saying they were bullied off the air by the homosexual agenda because they are Christians.

I have been looking for evidence of that bullying. Usually some group or organization is named as the culprit. It was not until last night I learned identity of these bullies. Benham said that after the show was announced in New York, "that's when the blogging began." Then referring to HGTV, Benham said: "They got bullied." This made me sit up, take notice, and ask myself, "How can bloggers bully?"

As a blogger, albeit small time, I have spent a decade spilling my thoughts and facts – that I feel are well researched – onto the web. I'm sure I have spoken negatively about many people or groups for something they said or did. Could anything I ever wrote be considered bullying? Of course not.

If HGTV executives changed their mind because of information they gathered from bloggers it can in no way be considered bullying. Even if the blogged information was wrong, in the end it's still an HGTV decision. If the blogs in question had slanderous information then the brothers can go after them in litigation. From what I've seen the blogs simply quoted the brother's words or those of their father.

David and Jason Benham are making the media tour presenting themselves as a victim of bloggers, while saying they aren't claiming victim status. If people like me are the new bullies – then I say welcome to the brave new world. As long as free speech and the Internet exists, people like myself will exist. We will sometimes write, some with bias, and even make mistakes. We will sometimes be wrong or misinterpret facts, but in no way can the blogger ever be called a bully.

The brothers appear to be conservative so should act like one. They do say they stand by their words and wish HGTV well, yet they place blame on bloggers who operate under the

1st Amendment. I'm sure their victim status will lead them to a bigger and better television gig.

They also blame the cancellation on the homosexual agenda. I know a heck of a lot of gay people and they all want only one thing, to be treated equally under the law. They want to live their lives with the people they love and have a government that doesn't tax and regulate them differently. I have written about the progressive agenda that does sometimes operate under the homosexual label. In this case it's not even those who are to blame.

The brothers cannot blame anyone other than themselves. They, like others, don't seem capable of understanding how their words sound to the average gay person. Phil Robertson made the same mistake as the Benham brothers. When you compare the homosexual to rapists and murders you cannot then turn and embrace them.

David and Jason Benham, here is my bullying to you. You are free in America to say whatever you please about whomever. You will also suffer the consequences of your words. When you say a negative and then a positive about someone in the same sentence, one doesn't counteract the other. Words have meaning and stand alone. As long as you speak out and compare gays to rapist, pedophiles, and murders, expect to be bullied by bloggers and many others in society.

The 1st Amendment empowers Americans the right to speak freely, but speech is rarely free – there is always a price. When I write I will be embraced by some and shouted at angrily by others. I know well the price of speech. You just learned your price.

The mistake of government controlled morality

Published on
3/20/14 2:33 PM

The Teatarian

I've written often about the word *moral*. I've talked about how it is too often used to support an argument. The definition of moral changes along with ideology and regional location. If you ask a progressive to give an example, they will likely tell you that it's immoral for someone to be obese. If you ask a conservative about sex outside of marriage they will tell you it's immoral. If marriage is sanctified by a government representative versus a minister, are they moral equals to the Christian?

Morality has always been a social institution. In the USA, what is considered immoral in the south is often more accepted in the north or west. In America's past it wasn't immoral to marry a 12 year old girl, while in today's society that is absolutely unacceptable. In those times life was about surviving. Male children were thought to be more capable at cutting firewood and plowing fields, while too often the female child was seen as simply another mouth to feed.

Female children were married off at or near puberty. Sometimes much older males would pay a diary for the right to marry that child. Arranged marriages are still happening around the world. Some of it might be for the same reasons as in our past, while in many cases it happens simply because it is now a tradition – just the way things are done.

Social standards evolve for a variety of reasons. In the modern American society arranged marriages are seen as barbaric. In today's world sex outside of marriage is much more common. In the not so distant past sex for women outside of marriage was forbidden while for men it was simply frowned upon. This is likely because it is the female that often bore the consequences for these liaisons. Out of wed births often stigmatized the woman and was too often a financial burden that was impossible to overcome. These pregnancies were also a barrier to future relationships. In short, the price for sex outside of marriage was too high. Because of science out of wedlock births are less likely to occur. While the financial burden for out of wedlock births are still a problem, it doesn't carry the social stigma of the past.

There is a major change that happened in modern societies. Throughout history it was society that decided these matters. This is how it should be because what might be a social problem for one village, might not be for another. Most modern Americans want government to control moral positions. History tells us that many thought Africans were not human, which made it acceptable to enslave them.

Many think that if the majority feels something isn't socially acceptable then it should be banned by government. There are those who would gladly imprison gays like it's done in other countries around the world. Thankfully, those people are not the majority in the USA. It is for this reason morality can't be a democratic decision.

The talk of today is about Duke University student, Belle Knox, who decided to pay her way through college by becoming a porn actress. You can imagine how her life has been transformed by this becoming common knowledge. Many conservatives are condemning her for this choice. This might not the the best life decision she will ever make, but it is one that should at least be noted as economically wise. She will graduate from a top university with no debt and with the satisfaction of not having taken money she didn't earn.

Belle might have found an unexpected benefit from her choice that could possibly end her short porn career. She is becoming a media darling, not because of her job, but for her political awareness. She is a self professed libertarian forced by the system to be Republican. I can tell her that she has a lot of company.

If American social standards hadn't evolved she would likely have been baring children by the time she was 15. Belle is teaching America that a few cannot sit in moral judgment of the world. Her decision could ultimately be a huge mistake, but it is one she is allowed make in a free society. We often learn best through our mistakes. If we let government control every aspect of our lives where small mistakes land us in prison or jail, then we might not learn the ultimate lesson that life can often teach. It has become clear that prison and fines do little to nothing for changing social standards. Drug prohibition has done nothing to lower crime, and might have even been behind its increase. As drug laws have begun to relax, violent crime has also decline.

Drugs, prostitution, fatty foods, salt on food, and gay marriage are all social issues that moralist want government to control or ban. The moralist are on both ends of the political spectrum. In my political ideology chart I placed libertarianism on the far right. If what I just said is true then libertarianism might be center or moderate.

It's expected when leftist want government control of everything they dislike, but it seems out of place when those calling for less government want the same thing, except in different areas. The most used argument for government control is that certain actions by people indirectly effect everyone else. If this is the case, then the government should just give us a daily list of activities that's acceptable because so many things we do indirectly effects others. It is for this reason we can only allow government to control actions that directly affect others, such as crimes like murder and robbery. No one will argue that either of those things should be allowed – except for anarchists.

I doubt you can find people on either the left or right that don't believe government is corrupt and can be bought by the highest bidder. Imagine a country where control of your daily decisions, something as simple as the food you eat, can be bought by the highest bidder. The highest bidder can make sure a dangerous drug is approved by the FDA. The next time you ask government to control morality, another liberty is lost. All rights are innate, even the ones with which you disagree.

Government can only remove rights, they cannot be given.

The Moral Atheist

Published on
5/20/13 10:22 AM

Each day we are all faced with moral decisions. We see this word tossed around by all people, but is there a single definition of morality? Christians see gay marriage as a moral issue because it goes against their religious teachings. The bible tells us about many things that mankind shouldn't do, which are labeled immoral.

If morality is based on religion, then that means non Christians can't be moral. That would mean those who came before Christianity couldn't be moral, yet they were. It's for this reason we must define morality.

Since mankind became a social creature they seemed to have lived under certain rules. If everyone stole from one another the social order would quickly break down. The same thing could be said for murder. Morality seems to come down to protecting possessions and family.

You are standing in line at the DMV and someone bumps into you accidentally several times. You become fed up and kick the person in the shin. Which act was immoral? Of course it is the kicking. Instead of kicking the bumper you become angry and kick your own shin. Is that immoral? Of course it isn't even if it might be extremely stupid.

Would cutting off your own hand be considered immoral? Under the Christian doctrine that forbids doing harm to ones self, then it would be immoral. In a non Christian society it might be seen simply as a mental deformity. In today's society many practice self mutilation in the form of tattoos, piercings, and body modifications. We could spend hours discussing the mental reasons, but I only ask – is it immoral? Some believe being gay or transgendered is immoral. Neither of those things harms anyone. There is even no apparent harm to themselves, yet both are often ostracized by some members of society because they see the acts as immoral.

Sometimes just being different can can create a perception of immorality. Even in today's world some will say it's immoral for those of different races to marry. The biracial children from such a marriage could be, and sometimes are, stigmatized by society. The children are the only moral argument. In the end, that could be considered a moral dilemma. In a free society government doesn't interfere with interracial relationships, even if a moral argument can be made.

For many, one of the the greatest sins, or moral atrocity, is to have sex outside of marriage. What harm does this bring? As long as it's practiced carefully it should bring none. Morality only comes into play if pregnancy arises from that coupling. At that moment a third, non-consenting party becomes involved. There then becomes a moral duty to care for that child. If one of the people involved in this relationship is married, then that relationship falls under the moral umbrella because there is another third, non-consenting party that will suffer; the non consenting spouse.

I only bring this up because I am seeing the word *moral* used a lot by those on the right. For those who view the term as I do, then they think little of its use. But there are those who shrink away when they see the word **moral** glaring at them like the preacher on Sunday morning after you had stolen your sister's ice cream cone. If we want others to hear our messages we must make them feel welcomed and eager to hear what we have to say. People don't want to be judged for their every perceived mistake in life. Morality is seen differently by many people. Most people just want to know what can be done to fix government while not having to sit in judgment of their peers.

The question was asked if the federal government should legislate morality. There was a resounding no, with only a few moralist who believed it was a duty of the federal government. So let's ask the same of state government. If we are going to give government the power to legislate morality, we must first define the term. Let's begin with biblical morality. The bible is clear that it's a sin to do harm to one's self.

Bloomberg is attempting to pass laws to prevent people from harming themselves in a variety of ways. He has placed limits and bans on foods such as hydrogenated oils, salt, and foods containing sugar. Is he obligated by morality to make these laws? I'll bet most on the right will say no, while those on the left will say yes.

It can be argued that by people eating unhealthy and living unhealthy lifestyles, that places a fiscal burden on others. It is an undeniable truth unhealthy lifestyles drive up health costs. If we are going to allow government to legislate morality, then we should be prepared to accept Bloomberg type laws in our own communities and states. By my own definition, it is only when something directly affects someone else that it is considered immoral. To stop Bloomberg type laws we must redefine morality to whatever directly effects someone else.

We must always be careful when we give government power because some individual will at some point come along and use those laws in ways we never imagined. What's moral to one person is immoral to another. Morality is relative to the perspective. What happens when you give the government power over morality and then one day your form of morality is a minority, while Bloomberg's is the majority?

Government Control

Stop and Frisk—The Police State

Published on
8/22/13

I first apologize that this might get lengthy because of quotes. Please bear with me because this might be one of the most important legal arguments this country faces today. New York city has a law named Stop and Frisk. It seems this law allows police to randomly stop people with suspicion of possessing a gun and frisk the surface area – outside clothing – of the person. Many of us believe this law comes into conflict with the 4th Amendment, which states that police must have reasonable cause to search Americans without a warrant and protects against unreasonable searches. I guess the first thing we must do is understand the difference between the two words.

> *From Dictionary.com:*
> *reasonable □(rea·son·a·ble) [ree-zuh-nuh-buhl, reez-nuh-]*
> *adjective*
> *1. agreeable to reason or sound judgment; logical: a reasonable choice for chairman.2.not exceeding the limit prescribed by reason; not excessive: reasonable terms.*
> *3.moderate, especially in price; not expensive: The coat was reasonable but not cheap.*
> *4.endowed with reason.*
> *5.capable of rational behavior, decision, etc.*
>
> *prob·a·ble [prob-uh-buhl] adjective*

1.likely to occur or prove true: He foresaw a probable business loss. He is the probable writer of the article.
2.having more evidence for than against, or evidence that inclines the mind to belief but leaves some room for doubt.
3.affording ground for belief.

un·rea·son·a·ble [uhn-ree-zuh-nuh-buhl, -reez-nuh-]
1.not reasonable or rational; acting at variance with or contrary to reason; not guided by reason or sound judgment; irrational: an unreasonable person.
2.not in accordance with practical realities, as attitude or behavior; inappropriate: His Bohemianism was an unreasonable way of life for one so rich.
3.excessive, immoderate, or exorbitant; unconscionable: an unreasonable price; unreasonable demands.
4.not having the faculty of reason.

4th Amendment
The right of the people to be secure in their persons, houses, papers, and effects, against unreasonable searches and seizures, shall not be violated, and no Warrants shall issue, but upon probable cause, supported by Oath or affirmation, and particularly describing the place to be searched, and the persons or things to be seized

The basis of the Stop and Frisk law stems from an incident in Ohio that eventually led to a 1968 Supreme Court decision. In short, a police detective saw John Terry and another guy standing in front of a store. The men appeared to be casing the store for a potential robbery. These men were approached by the detective and frisked. John Terry was arrested on a gun charge.

Stop and Frisk according to the online law dictionary:
stop and frisk n. a law enforcement officer's search for a

weapon confined to a suspect's outer clothing when either a bulge in the clothing or the outline of the weapon is visible. The search is commonly called a "pat down," and any further search requires either a search warrant or "probable cause" to believe the suspect will commit or has committed a crime (including carrying a concealed weapon, which itself is a crime). The limited right to "stop and frisk" is intended to halt the practice of random searches of people in hopes of finding evidence of criminal activity or merely for purposes of intimidation, particularly of minorities.

I dare say the detective was correct and these men were likely up to no good. In this case the detective might have had reasonable cause and was not unreasonable in their pat-down of the men that led to finding the weapon. What has puzzled me is if an officer operates within the 4th Amendment, why do you need a specialized Stop and Frisk law?

Some don't like the law because they say it targets minorities and there is some evidence that can support the belief. The police are also targeting high crime areas, which is largely minority. Let's not concentrate on the racial aspects, but what makes this law so different from normal police operating procedures. In NYC they say they are doing these random searches to remove guns from the street. If this is the case we must look at another SCOTUS decision.

The Court somewhat retreated from their John Terry decision in *Florida v. J. L.* (U.S. 2000), in which it ruled that an anonymous tip identifying a person who is carrying a gun is not, without more reason, sufficient to justify a police officer's stop and frisk of that person. The U.S. Supreme Court concluded that the tip, stating that a young black male was standing at a particular bus stop, wearing a plaid shirt, and carrying a gun, lacked sufficient reliability to provide reasonable suspicion to make a Terry stop.

It would appear that if we leave these decisions to a

policeman's reasonable belief, we are opening ourselves up to severe infringement of the 4th Amendment. For that reason we must look at the entire Amendment and not a few words. It states that *the right of the people to be secure in their persons, houses, papers, and effects, against unreasonable searches and seizures.* We know that the police must be careful when entering a house. They usually are very sure there is an ongoing crime, or they ask for permission to enter the home. If permission is denied they might seek a warrant.

Our persons should garner the same respect under the law as our home. SCOTUS rules that a simple pat down, such as the ones by the TSA in airports is not a search. I beg to differ and the difference between TSA pat-downs and one by a police officer on the street, is permission. By knowing we could possibly be patted down while boarding a plane, we give implied permission. The same applies if you knowingly go into an event that has a security line. Merely walking down the street offers no implied consent.

When self proclaimed conservatives and libertarians argue Stop and Frisk makes the city safer, they have just crossed over to the left where police states lie. The Constitution doesn't guarantee safety—only liberty

Here is the statistic for which I've been looking. According to the New York Times only 6% of the stops resulted in guns being found. This tells me the searches weren't reasonable under the concept of the 4th Amendment. I would say that the stops versus guns found should average above 50% for the majority of the searches to be reasonable.

The Times also stated that for every 100 individuals stopped and frisked, only about 6% were arrested, and most of those were for minor offenses such as marijuana possession. The report stated that only 1 of every 1000 stops produced a gun. It has been said that randoms stops often produce better results because police don't want to risk violating 4th Amendment rights. Without the protection of Stop and Frisk laws the officer seems to look for actual evidence instead of frivolously searching individuals.

In one year New York City officers stopped 46,784 woman and frisked nearly16,000. Guns were found in only 59 cases, according to police statistics. The number of women stopped in 2011 represented 6.9% of all police stops. The rate of guns found on both men and women was equally low, only 0.12% and 0.13% respectively. The low numbers can in no way be seen as a justification for the law, or the police officer's actions.

Now that you have been presented with all the facts, how do you feel about such laws and searches?

The UFO Syndrome

Published on
1/20/13 8:39 AM

I want to begin by saying this isn't about UFOs and space aliens. What it is about is our government and how it controls speech. It began one night in 1947 Roswell, New Mexico where something crashed in the desert. After discovery of the craft, the local paper's headlines were about some type of aircraft crash. The government seemed to be talking openly about the unidentified craft. Then something suddenly happened, the crash became a weather balloon, none at the scene were allowed to talk.

In time, stories began to spread about what had happened that day. The government turned these stories into a joke, laughing at them. In time the government laughed at anyone who talked of anything flying that couldn't be defined, whether it be extraterrestrial or secret government programs. The government had discovered the greatest disinformation tool possible, mockery. The media was all too happy to join in because they feared being mock themselves. They had a reputation to maintain.

Today the UFO syndrome is in full effect. When someone asks about Obama's college or birth records they are mocked and ridiculed. All of the major media figures became afraid to broach the subject. There is something even more recent. During one of the debates Mitt Romney talked about the threat of Al Qaeda in Mali. The president actually laughed at the candidate and went on to express how he had defeated Al Qaeda. I believe this was important to him winning the election. We know today that Romney was correct in his statements about Mali, where Al Qaeda is alive and strong.

When we ask about the death of an ambassador we are told it's nothing, this kind of thing happens. We are told they know the risk when going into these countries. What they don't tell is that it's been thirty years since an ambassador was killed. We are dismissed offhandedly when asking questions or presenting facts.

We know thousands of people are sneaking across the border in the dark of night. Some of those are people simply looking for a better life, while some are gun runners, drug dealers, kidnappers, and Islamic terrorists. When we speak out about this problem we are called xenophobes and racist. We are ridiculed just as those who see lights in the sky at night. We are not allowed to care that a country should have secure borders and the right to know who enters and leaves. They fight us by controlling the language.

The UFO syndrome is alive and well in the debate over the 2nd Amendment. For claiming the rights afforded us by our fore fathers we are called extremist and lovers of death. When we protest and tell the left we need weapons to protect us from government, we are mocked and laughed at while telling us we cannot stop tanks with rifles. I believe we should be allowed to possess many of the same weapons as the government, but it doesn't take them to defend ourselves. Francis Marion defeated one of the greatest British armies with almost nothing. The Afghanistans defeated the mighty Russian military. The USA is the longest sustaining democracy with a peaceful transition of power. This didn't happen despite guns, but because of them. Disinformation and fear tactics are the only tools the left has against the 2nd Amendment.

The right is mocked when we talk about lowering taxes and limiting the size of the federal government. We are called extremist because we want to returned the country to what was envisioned by the founders. We are ridiculed for believing the Constitution isn't an outdated document.

We are laughed at for not believing Franklin D. Roosevelt was the greatest president ever. I will give him credit for winning World War 2. I will give him discredit for imprisoning the country in the worst economic period ever, yet by history he is praised for his work in the Great Depression. He is praised for the New Deal, while we are ridiculed for pointing out the truth, that his progressive policies locked the country in poverty. We can point to how Keynesian economics almost destroyed the country, yet we are mocked and call voodoo economist for believing in proven supply side economics.

When we talk about communists we're mocked and ridiculed. Those mockers won't stop to tell you that we speak about an ideological belief that government should own and run all businesses. This belief is becoming more common in the USA. They want you to believe we are wrapped in a veil of paranoia and chasing some invisible Russian or Chinese.

I can go on and on with item after item where the opposition is ridiculed. No one wants to be mocked so they will many times publicly agree with something, while quietly having reservations. There is also the fact that some can't believe the ridiculed can be correct. The mockers appear to be the one with the high ground and knowledge. They toss around disinformation as fact, and statistics as if it was confetti at a celebration.

The UFO syndrome is an effective tactic that will be used for as long as man lives. It was later indirectly wrote about in *Rules for Radicals*, as well as Edward Bernays' books on propaganda and modern marketing. So far no one has found a weapon against the UFO Syndrome, but one had better come soon or we have lost. Only when the country lies in ashes created by progressive policies will we be proven correct. By then it might be too late.

UFO Syndrome – Ducking the Truth

Published on
1/2/14 4:13 PM

In UFO Syndrome I spoke to how government uses language to control the actions and beliefs of others. We should thank Edward Bernays, the father of modern day marketing and propaganda for the world in which we live today. Bernays used the woman's suffrage movement to sell cigarettes to women. He helped elect presidents. Well placed marketing can affect millions of people.

Recently there was Duck Dynasty-gate where the patriarch of the family said some things against gays and blacks that made A&E place Phil Robertson on hiatus. This coincided with with the Christmas holiday Duck Dynasty marathon. Viewership for the marathon dropped 71% compared to the previous week. We will never know if it was simply because they were reruns, it was the holidays, or because of the boycott against A&E for their actions. For the purpose of this writing it doesn't matter.

We might never know how this worked out for A&E, but I saw something important when it came to the Robertson family. Many rallied around the family and began defending them as if they were their own. Those who said anything close to negative about the Robertsons was attacked. What we witnessed was the power of television, marketing, and of words.

People attach themselves to others who are total strangers – be it a sick girl in a hospital, a German family, or a wealthy Louisiana business men. Everyone is seeking a victim for whom they can support and protect. This is an instinct of humankind. This protection can extended to politicians who are portrayed as victims. We saw that with Ted Cruz as he was attacked, even by his own side, for his hours long filibuster. It didn't matter that in the end he accomplished little other than gain a dedicated following. Was this simply a political stunt? It doesn't matter for purpose of the UFO Syndrome. It matters only that it worked to improve his popularity.

No matter if you are Democrat, Republican, conservative, or libertarian, we are all humans and most will react the same. When we are are shown photos of starving inner city children, the first reaction is to help. The disagreement always comes with how to help. It is there that people are purposely divided. This is how people fall under effect of the UFO Syndrome. Government, along with politicians, all shout they have the solutions. We know they don't because poverty is at an all time high. Despite poverty numbers people still follow governmental promises.

There is an animation where people are following one another into a dark hole. There are experiments that indicate the animation isn't very disconnected from reality. Test have shown how people will follow signs or lines even when they are led in a circle. Children who have been taught to never go with strangers will follow them if it's to help find a poor lost dog. Seven of nine children went with the stranger in a British experiment.

In most scenarios a few people will step out as leaders, while the rest are content to follow. No one wants to be mocked as being dumb or pointed to as lacking compassion.

This isn't something that's been taught to us in life, but an instinct that is as much a part of us as our skin. I've made the comment that Washington and those who follow reminded me a lot of high school. This is because there are driving instincts that we will never outgrow.

No matter the political side of your choice it's taken for the same reason – the need to care. Each side sees themselves as caring the most. Government knows this and will use it to its gain. Government uses this knowledge to keep us divided. They use it as a tool to hide their secrets and mistakes. When a mistake or secret by government escapes we begin to hear conspiracy theories. Government knows all that's needed is to plant a seed of tainted truth and it will sprout into a full blow conspiracy. There are those who have gotten rich growing conspiracies. This is no different from those who have made a career of nurturing racism.

Unless you are fully aware, and even then there is a possibility you will succumb to the UFO Syndrome. You will find yourself carrying the water just as was planned by those in, or wanting, power. Government will seduce you by playing to your nurturing instinct. We have those news sources we see as reliable, but we must remember that even they can fall prey to instincts. Even journalists are humans first.

This leaves us with deciding when we are under influence of the UFO Syndrome. We can never be absolutely sure, but we must question everything. Never fully trust anyone who wants your money or vote. There is always someone out there telling you what you need or want to hear. There is always someone ready to sell it to you. Government, politics, and marketing are no different.

They have come at us with our own history books. They are typically based on fact, but the stories have been distorted to favor a particular side. Remember the old adage, history is always told by the victor. In former Confederate states we were taught history from books written by those in the victorious

North. Those text books differ from those in Canada and history as passed down from our southern parents.

History paints the picture of a government that saved millions of people from starvation during the Great Depression. History books and its tellers fail to tell how it was government that caused the poverty and helped preserve that poverty for a decade. Only those aware of the UFO syndrome will search for the the truths not recorded in official history. While searching for that truth beware of the rabbit hole, for there are many.

Disaster – Government Control of Drugs

Published on
4/25/14 5:25 PM

As election time nears, discussions of Marijuana legalization or decriminalization heats up. We see leading prospective 2016 president wannabes such as Governors Christie and Perry expressing their views on Marijuana. Their views are likely to represent the GOP pack, and likely some of the Democratic candidates

> *"Gov. Chris Christie says he will 'never' permit legalized marijuana use while he's the governor of New Jersey "*

He and others cite a study that casual marijuana use could be detrimental to the human brain. This study could be correct, but the effects of drugs on the human biology plays no part in this writing. There are many things legal that do great harm to our bodies, such as smoking tobacco and alcohol use topping the list. Efforts to ban either of those go nowhere. In fact, crime became so prevalent because of alcohol prohibition that an Amendment was passed to once again allow sale.

T. L. Crain

Christie also said: "I am not going to be the governor who's going to tell our children and our young adults that marijuana use is okay. Because it's not."

While politicians are debating an innocuous drug like marijuana we stand idly by as children are turned into addicts. The greatest number of addicts aren't buying their drugs from scurrilous dealers on the corner, but from those dressed in white with magical prescription pads. Our greatest number of addicts aren't a result of illegal drugs, but those tightly controlled by the federal government. Parents fear sending their children to the seedy side of town where you find drug dealers, but they will gladly push them into the waiting arms of the drug pusher wearing white – the drug dealer who was given power by the state.

I need to establish this is not all doctors and that some are only doing what they are taught best by government controlled universities. Even doctors with the best intentions can create addicts. I know, because I grew up with one of those addicts. The sad fact was that no one realized at the time her problems were a result of drugs prescribed by an all knowing doctor.

I would love to say that at least with drug dealers being government representatives that removes the criminal element. In fact, the opposite is true. A system has been created where pharmaceutical companies will take great extremes to have their drugs approved. Too often we hear where people die because a drug was approved too soon, or die because government refused to approve a drug. Occasionally we hear about someone flying to another country for treatment that's not approved in the USA. The left is always telling us the wealthy have an unfair advantage. In this type of instance that does appear to be the case.

We have two avenues for drug distribution, one filled with street crime and the other other filled with white collar crime.

We must ask, which is the worse? I'm not sure there is a lot of difference except white collar crime is well hidden from public eyes and less likely to be prosecuted.

What's the difference between a heroin addict and a Dilaudid addict? The difference is the dealer. One might wear a hoodie while the other a white doctor's coat. We all know drug abuse destroys lives no matter the source.

All we have to do is turn on the television to find a stream of pharmaceutical advertisements. While the picture is one of tranquility and soothing music, we are bombarded with a list of deadly side effects. The fact these ads are on televisions tell us they work. Despite the long list of potentially deadly side effects, people clamber to their doctor asking for these drugs.

People will seek ways to escape life no matter how much force government uses. Government cannot ban chemistry and the long list of chemical combinations that can be turned into drugs. Many of those combinations are much more dangerous than those provided naturally by nature. The war on drugs has done almost nothing to slow drug use. If nothing else it might be the cause of more addicts because people will seek out legal prescription drugs.

It sickens me when I see Republicans like Chris Christie play the child card as an excuse to continue drug prohibition. Democrats have been slammed for decades for telling us we need laws because it's to keep the kids safe. To even say they want to stop drug use to prevent crime is a misnomer. In some of the mildest suburban neighborhoods drug use is rampant, yet they have little or no crime. Politicians are using age old fear tactics to help maintain the police state.

Recently I was talking to my friend about being robbed. The police were useless. They made no effort to find the robber despite the fact he just left my premises. I live three miles from the sheriff's department, which tells me their arrival couldn't have taken long. I was even holding someone who might have been involved, but he was not even detained. My friend suggested that I should have told them I thought they had drugs to spur them into action.

If my incident had involved drugs that could have padded their statistics to receive more state and federal funds, which would have spurred them to action. The drug war is a source of funding for law enforcement. With any matter we have only to follow the money to find the truth.

In states that are dominated by the Democratic Party, drug legalization has moved at a snail's pace – often at best all that gets passed is medicinal Marijuana. On the right we have those who shout angrily about the encroaching police state and how the war on drugs is at the root. Yet they will then turn around and preach the evils of marijuana and fight legalization. Left or right they talk a big game, but there is little action. Even those citizens behind marijuana legalization will often balk at ending drug prohibition.

As long as we continue playing the politician's game we will forever be the pawn. The only way to win this game is to stop playing. Prohibition has been proven to not work. Banning guns doesn't end gun violence. Banning drugs only creates more gun violence. The only way to get the criminal drug dealer off the streets peddling to your children is to give the income to legitimate business owners who will protect your children. At one time we had people dying from moonshine made in stills with lead laden car radiators. Would you feel safer buying that next drink from a toxic still or the bartender in the local pub? Drugs are no different. Too often the danger of snorting cocaine is the base compound with which it's cut, and not the drug itself.

Slavery, Yesterday and Today

Published on
12/25/13 9:33 AM

The Teatarian

I was just reminded about Irish slavery, something about which history rarely speaks. Slavery is alive and well in today's world. We all know about Uganda slaves, but the largest slave market might currently be the one for women and children. This is typically known as the white slave or sex trade.

I can never forget the tale of a Russian teen during the 90's. She had dreams of being a European model. The young beauty signed with some company and managed a visa to leave Russia. She arrived at the address given to her and was immediately taken into captivity. For some time she was used as a prostitute in Europe. She was eventually sold to someone in the USA. Her captives planned to bring her through the southern border with fake documentation.

She sat nervously in the back seat as they were questioned at a border checkpoint. One of the border guards finally looked at her paperwork and ask the Russian captive a question. Despite speaking fluent English, she decided to reply in Russian. The cold war was still fresh enough in everyone's mind that this made them look more closely at her and the paperwork. The guards took her from the car to some place where she could be questioned alone. It was then she revealed to them who she was and that she had been kidnapped. The kidnappers were arrested and and she was given asylum in the USA.

Inspiration for this article came from a photo . It said that, "blacks should stop whining over slavery." This seems to have created a firestorm of controversy. There has been a long history of slavery for people of all races. We all know about the Jewish history of slavery. From 1641 to 1652, over 500,000 Irish were killed by the English – 300,000 more were sold into slavery. During the 1650's, over 100,000 Irish children between the ages of 10 and 14 were ripped from their homes and sold as slaves to West Indies, Virginia, and New England.

I could go on and on about how people of all colors have

been persecuted or sold into slavery. The hard part is lifting ourselves out of a repressive history and making sure it never happens again. No particular slavery was worse than that of another. What's important is living in a country being torn apart by two very different ideologies. Those ideologies are made up of people with a history of slavery and that of the slave owner.

Everyone is grasping for leverage. They yield their history like a sword in defense of a government that was once the slave master. No government is innocent when it comes to slavery. In some ways government is still trying to be the slave master. It wants to control people and the wages they earn. That government imports illegal labor to work fields and to manicure the lawns in front of their mansions.

Slavery could have never existed in the USA and much of the world save for one thing – government. Think of any ill in the world today or in the past and you will find government in the picture. Sometimes government is heavily involved, or it simply turns a blind eye to evils done by the favored.

Cronyism is out of control in the USA. No matter if that government is a majority of Democrats or Republicans. Today the Affordable Care Act is the most important topic of the century. The ACA is also the biggest act of cronyism the country has ever seen. When government mandates a citizen buy a product from a private company we have truly become an Oligarchy, or at least a fascist nation.

Unless we can stop arguing over history and try to fix the world around us, we might all become slaves. When government decides what we eat, what we must buy, and decide how much we are paid – when government controls every aspect of our lives we have become slaves and Washington the slave master. It seems staggering that people can actually elect their own slave masters, yet we may be doing just that. When government can be sold to the highest bidder, those doing the buying become the slave masters.

You can place all your faith in Democrats or Republicans, but both seek to be the slave master. Our founders feared a central power. All we have to do is look at the history of slavery to see why that fear was well founded. Because states were allowed to self govern there were free states to which slaves could flee.

In states that allowed slavery the owners were the rich and influential. They controlled government for their own financial gain. It was cronyism that allowed slavery to exist. As long as we side with acts of cronyism we are once again risking the possibility of slavery. We might receive a weekly check, but that doesn't remove the possibility of being a slave to government. It's time to stop being a slave to the two main political parties. Have courage and remove them from power. We must never forget that the only person who can allow us to become a slave is our self.

Wikileaks – Accident, Plan, or Ineptitude?

Published on
11/28/10 1:45 PM

We now have Wiki Leaks telling us they are going to release private State Department communications. The website is already filled with 350mb of supposed sensitive military material. This tells me we have a serious problem within our government.

We have the TSA controversy with body scanners filling the news. Our government assures us that these images cannot be saved or transmitted. We are already seeing images appear on Gizmodo. Time and time again the government reassures us that something is safe, only later to find that we had been swept up into a false sense of security. The only way we can assure privacy is to take it into our own hands. This also applies to our medical records. Once we let the federal government place them in some central database, we no longer have control.

The government is proving with these latest leaks that they cannot secure even embarrassing communications. There is another possibility, and that's these communications are being intentionally leaked. It's clear that the progressives don't much like this country and relish any opportunity to see it embarrassed.

I have the impression that at least some of these communications contain embarrassing remarks about the Chinese leadership. China holds the majority of our debt. Is it possible Obama wants to anger the Chinese so much that they will stop buying our debt, which will further collapse the dollar?

I don't yet have enough information to make a judgment as to what's really happening. I do know that when it comes to politicians, things rarely happen by accident. The leaks on the wars were clearly to discredit Bush and the Republicans.

Our government has the ability to steal our emails and to monitor our financial transactions, but they can't find a foreign server transmitting sensitive documents and shut it down. There is more to this than meets the eye. Is our government truly this inept? If they are, where is the media asking the government hard questions and holding them accountable? Oh yes, silly me, it's a democratic controlled government. The left trusts government implicitly as long as it's their party in control. Many on the right are no different when it comes to trusting their own party when in charge.

The War on Monsanto

Published on
12/7/13 1:16 PM

154

The Teatarian

Most days I get at least one tweet or Facebook post telling me about the evils of Monsanto and GMO (Genetically Modified Organisms). It usually accompanies a link to one of the conspiracy sites. When I research something I look for education websites or trusted journalist. I have spent the past decade trying to learn as much as possible about climate change. I must admit that I haven't put as much time into researching Genetically Modified Organisms. I do try to understand enough to know if the foods I'm eating are killing me. I'm sure most things we do in life affect life span in some way.

The one thing we know for certain is that people are living longer than ever. We also know that's mostly due to hygiene, medical care, home environment, and an abundance of food. I'm sure most of us learned in history about the 1930's dust bowl. That was when a large portion of the plains states were trapped in a cloud of dust because of bad farming techniques and a drought.

A dust bowl of today is much less likely, not because there aren't droughts, but because of better farming techniques and drought resistant crops. Some of those crops are a result of hybridization and some from genetic modification. Because of hybridization and genetic modifications we can grow far more food per acre than in the dust bowl era.

Hybridization has been done for thousands of years. It is through the hybridizing process that we have those Granny Sweets. For most of history apples were used only for cider because they were too sour for table fruit. A farmer could grow a thousand trees and only a few would have sweet apples suitable for eating off the tree. Farmers began to save the seeds from those sweet apples and grow only those. Problem solved, right? No. If you replant seeds from the same plant over and over the fruit will get smaller and eventually stop producing. To solve this problem farmers grafted parts of the sweet trees

155

to those that produce sour apples. After about a thousand years of this process we now have an abundance and a large variety of sweet apples. This is an over implication, but it gives you an idea about the process.

Modern science discovered a way, through genetic manipulation, to duplicate the process that sometimes took a thousand years. Science on the genetic level is relatively safe. Until the learning curve is straightened out there are risk. We have always heard that without great risk there are no rewards.

Today, when we see the outcry over GMO, we must ask which one. It seems the one that most worries people is the addition of the bacteria Bt *(Bacillus thuringiensis)* that is a natural pesticide. The biggest danger found so far is the killing of Monarch Butterflies in proximity to fields.

We know there are many insecticides that are reasonably safe for humans, but deadly to insects. Because of insecticides we have greatly reduced crop loss that allows more people to be fed from less land use. Less crop loss keeps food prices low, making it more affordable to the poor.

Monsanto has a long history of government cronyism. That fact alone doesn't make them good or bad. We do know that cronyism interferes with the free market. Anytime a company gets special treatment it's not the American way. Environmental companies of today are getting huge subsidies. People often turn a blind eye to environmental cronyism while decrying Monsanto.

In politics we too often choose sides and defend them vigorously. When we do that we defend cronyism. We are hypocrites if we defend cronyism when it supports our favorite cause. The only way to solve the cronyism problem is to limit federal power in step 1. In step 2 we turn to our own states. Until we limit governmental power we will always have cronyism in some form. If you truly believe Monsanto is evil then the only way to prevent more of the same is to eliminate federal power.

Fighting the symptoms of a disease does little to cure the illness. We must stop forgiving broken promises. We have got to stop looking to government for solutions. Some believe the only way to control companies like Monsanto is with more government. That's like curing a broke leg by breaking the other.

Yes, this is the libertarian way at looking at a problem. It's also the way our founders looked at problems. They were men of the world and had seen countries rise and fall. They were well aware of what lay ahead for the United States. Despite that forewarning we have fallen into almost every trap they tried to avoid with the Constitution.

To lessen our fears of GMO we must stop putting our faith in government and then crying foul when it lets us down. Life offers no guarantees. If you want food labeling, then go to the retailers and demand it from them – not forced by government. This has worked well for organic foods. Almost every market has an organic foods section. There is a retailer that has placed it's business plan on the organic foods industry. I only ask that you have more faith in the free market than a government that has continuously let us down. Have more faith in yourself – the consumer – because in the end you hold all power over the market.

I should also remind you that because of cronyism and past ills, Monsanto has been labeled the enemy. There are many companies around the world that are doing much the same things, and there is silence. I only mention this so that you might stop and wonder why Monsanto is often the lone target.

Why Does Congress Not Read The Bills?

Published on
12/19/10 7:05 PM

The Democrats rolled out a 2000 page $1.1 trillion spending bill and tried to ram it through congress. They have no idea who wrote the bill – what's worse, they don't care. The people stood up and screamed when the Democrats did the same thing with the 2400 page health-care bill. It would take a team of lawyers months to just read these bills.

We now know the health-care bill had been written years before by the left wing Apollo Foundation to which Soros gives millions. Are we ever told by Congress who writes the bills? Do they expect Americans to be so gullible as to believe these bills were written that month? The Democrats have now been in power for four years. They have taken all this time to write, amend, or edit bills written by any number of organizations, and then waited for the waning days of the lame-duck Congress in which to ram these bills through. The Democrats wanted to be sure no one else had the time to read these bills.

These bills contain hundreds of references to other laws. When someone attempts to read a 2000 page bill, they must also read thousands of pages from current law. Knowing this, it's obvious these people are voting for bills of which they have no knowledge. They know only what they have been told by staffers. Congress is also aware these bills contain hundreds of pages of text that doesn't pertain to the debate at hand. They know the bills contain items that will severely cripple the rights of the individuals, all in the name of helping.

Nancy Pelosi said before the media, "We have to pass the bill to find out what's in it." That was probably the most honest she has ever been. Those that voted for obamacare are now learning that many of the fears had by detractors were true. Even many Democrats that supported the bill now believe portions should be repealed. There have been hundreds of exemptions issued to Democratic friendly companies and Unions.

Now we know for sure that Congress never reads, or has

little knowledge of these bills – then why do they vote for them? Why do they push them with such fervor? The answer is simple, they know it will further their ideological agenda. They know these bills come from groups in which they share ideology. They pass bills that were written in part by the Communist Party.

These bills come from people that care little for the Constitution and are one-world order organizations. They come from George Soros who runs the Open Society Foundation. Is this some secret conspiracy? No, these people operate in the open. They are a secret to many because most of the media will not tell the truth. They are often labeled by the mainstream media as a watchdog group.

Knowledge is power. As long as we know about these organizations and the intentions of those for which we vote, then we hold power over them. We the voters are the power. The next time a politician tells you that Americans must sacrifice, shout back that it's they who must sacrifice… read the bill. Once they are required to read the bills they might then decide it's time for plain English laws.

What happened to the 4th Amendment?

Published on
4/20/13 12:44 AM

For the last few days as I watched events unfold in Boston my mind was a jumble of thoughts. I watched as innocent people suffered at the hands of terrorists. I watched as Americans tried to rally against those terrorists who would make us afraid to leave our homes and to gather in mass to follow American traditions.

As time passed I watched the news and tried to pick real facts from a maze of distortions cast by the media and the police themselves. I cast no blame for that misinformation because I know some was done by accident and some for good intentions. I suspect it might be a long time before we have all the true facts of the story, and it's for that reason I tread lightly here.

I spent my life trying to understand the how and why of all things. In this search I have seen a lot of rights and wrongs. I have come to the conclusion that the greatest question we can ask is, what is right? There are many perceptions of right and wrong, of moral and immoral. Sometimes the path to enlightenment lies in the questions themselves. So let's ask some questions.

Who is correct, the political left or right? I think both sides are correct, but it's in the solutions where the differences lie. Not long after the Occupy Wall Street event I spent all night talking to both organizers and participants. I found them to be greatly divided on solutions, in part because that always happens and we all think differently. Part of the reason for their differences was that some of the organizers were out for power and money, while others were average citizens wanting a voice.

I find the same problems with the Tea Party movement. They all mostly agree on the problems, but the solutions differ. There is also the problem of those using the movement for power and money. It is because of those influences that both movements seem to have fallen apart. We love to use the term organic when it comes to political movements. That means it's pure of heart and from the people – not some powerful organization. No movement can stay organic for an extended period of time. What are the common problems found by both Occupy and the Tea Party? The answer is simple, government, it's association with corporations, and other supposed free market entities. Even though they see the same problem, their perceptions of the problems differ greatly. I think in the end both sides want plenty of government, but desire it to operate the way that best suits their world view.

Which side is correct? The answer is simple, neither. There is the old saying that power corrupts. That will forever hold true. The only way to rein in that corruption is to reduce power. The only way to reduce power is to operate with less government. The founders designed a formula where the country could operate on the edge of anarchy. Less government means the least corruption.

This would be a good time to explain how prohibition of anything only breeds corruption. Because of the war on drugs we have created the basis for a police state. But I don't want to talk about prohibition, I want to talk about terrorism. The object of terrorism is to create terror so that people can be manipulated by fear. Politicians use fear tactics to get certain laws passed. Others do it to push their ideological agenda.

There is good evidence that suggest the Boston bombing was done in the name of religion. Islamic terrorism is worldwide and a serious problem. I watch politicians standing in the bright glare of television lights declaring they are defeating the terrorists

Who is really winning the war on terrorism? The terrorist have won hands down. I didn't believe that until I watched the events unfold in Boston, Mass. I watched the police shut down a city of several million people. They told people to stay in their homes as hundreds or thousands of police, government agents, and military roamed the streets in search of a 19 year old teenager. Yes, he was heavily armed and dangerous, but don't all cities have these types of individuals? I watched as the police participated in running gun fights, and speeding car chases with guns a-blazing. I saw a city terrorized, but not by the 19 year old terrorist, but by police and media.

The people of Boston huddled in their homes afraid to venture out in their yards. I heard police admit to searching every house for several blocks, The police refused to trust the good citizens of Boston and assumed they were all assisting the terrorist. Why were military police on the streets of Boston? Where was habius corpus? Had martial law been declared? Where was the 4th Amendment?

> *Amendment IV*
> *The right of the people to be secure in their persons, houses, papers, and effects, against unreasonable searches and seizures, shall not be violated, and no Warrants shall issue, but upon probable cause, supported by Oath or affirmation, and particularly describing the place to be searched, and the persons or things to be seized.*

Was Boston a sign of the future for this country? There will be more terrorism. There will always be fanatics. Do we want to live in a police state that cannot guarantee terrorism will cease to exist? When Bush passed the Patriot Act that gave government expanded powers, the left and some on the right screamed in anger. When President Obama made the Patriot Act permanent, too many were silent. Our government has given itself the right to suspend the 4th Amendment whenever they utter the word terrorism.

Now I ask the biggest question of them all. Would you rather live in a country that might be a little dangerous, but where you have all your civil liberties and protections intact? Or do you want to live in a police state so that you feel safe?

We will all answer those questions by our actions, whether they be in the polling booth or by joining a political movement. I only ask that you think hard about how you answer those questions, because my freedoms and those of our children will be effected.

CBO And Other Spin

Published on
2/7/14 10:17 AM

The Teatarian

While listening to all the spin about the CBO report on people leaving their jobs voluntarily due to the availability of insurance. I must say that conservatives have taken the wrong road on this topic. During my 33 years of working I met many people who had after hours businesses of their own and worked the hourly job only for insurance.

I have also known people that would have retired early had it not been for insurance. People who have lived a thrifty life have set in place everything they need to exist outside a steady job. Some like myself chose this path in order pursue their dreams. I know of others who would, and have left to live off the meager income of their hobbies.

This doesn't justify federally subsidized insurance. This in no way defends any part of the ACA. But if it is the law and will potentially offer subsidized insurance, we must stick only to the facts. I believe in this case the democrats are correctly stating that some of those in the categories I mentioned above will leave their current jobs. This also doesn't mean they will stop working for others. They may simply work part time.

This will make full time positions available. No one in their right mind would say this is any kind of fix for shoring up the workforce. I suspect the numbers involved will be too negligible to matter. Some conservative commentators are saying some will leave the workforce for welfare. They could have done that before obamacare. To win this war me must fight the good battles and not grasp for every straw. There are too many real targets that can be attacked.

I wish there was some way to leave the workforce without taking great risk such as living with no insurance. If we fought and used the free market to bring insurance rates or healthcare cost down to an affordable rate for low level income earners, then more could pursue their dreams and possibly start the next 1000 employee company.

Obamacare is doing a good job tearing itself apart. Another

thing I learned a long time ago while working and that is people will accept a lot of crap from their employer. But if you mess with their insurance they turn into a pack of wolves. I knew that unless the ACA went into effect almost flawlessly America would turn on the government like that proverbial pack of wolves. They can paint that pig any color they want, but in the end it will still stink. For this reason the talking heads need to stick to obvious battles without trying to create problems where there aren't any.

We know the media is always looking for a new topic. Those people make their living talking. Sometimes their talking helps our cause, and sometimes they do great harm. For those of us who are little more than a voter we must be careful of what we echo. If we repeat something just because we heard our favorite talking head say it, then we might be doing our cause a terrible injustice. We must stay focused on the larger targets. The endgame is to shrink government, not making the democrats look bad. As we have often seen, if they are given enough rope they will hang themselves.

NSA spying—The modern Panopticon

Published on
9/26/13 9:45 AM

A panopticon is a prison design created by English philosopher and social theorist Jeremy Bentham in the late 18th century. The design was circular and allowed for prisoners to be in view at all times. His design allowed for the elimination of bars and locks. Bentham saw this form of imprisonment as mind on mind control. New prisons of today sometimes use the basic panopticon design.

There was an outcry about Bentham's design because the

prisoner never had privacy. Today we monitor prisoners 24/7 using CCTV cameras. Some still argue that watching people 24 hours a day is not healthy and possibly abuse. Today's prisons go even farther by placing RFIDs on prisoners so that if one wanders into an area off limits an alarm will activate.

Today we are living in a panopticon world. We have the NSA doing 24/7 surveillance of our communications. This isn't something new. It has come to light the NSA monitored notables such as Martin Luther King and Mohamed Ali. They weren't spied on because it was believed they were potential terrorists – it was simply because they spoke openly about their political beliefs.

It has also come to light that two sitting Senators were also under surveillance – the Idaho Democrat Frank Church and Howard Baker, a Republican from Tennessee who, puzzlingly, was a firm supporter of the war in Vietnam. They also monitored foreign communications of respected journalists, such as Tom Wicker of the New York Times and popular satirical writer for the Washington Post, Art Buchwald.

After exposure by NSA contractor Joesph Snowden, the agency has admitted to an effort which would result in gathering data and phone information on all Americans. At this time they admit the capability is limited to 75% of all citizens.

Almost every American has a cell phone and many of which have cameras. We now also have a growing number of smart televisions, laptops, and tablet computers in homes, many of which have microphones and video cameras. A hacker or the US government can activate any of these devices at any time. They can watch or listen even when the device is thought to be off.

This technology is tempting to law enforcement and government who has proven to be more aggressive than ever. Not long ago a court ruled that police and government couldn't use radar imaging to view Americans through rooftops without a warrant.

T. L. Crain

The right to privacy was so important to the founders it was mandated in the 4th Amendment:

Amendment IV

The right of the people to be secure in their persons, houses, papers, and effects, against unreasonable searches and seizures, shall not be violated, and no Warrants shall issue, but upon probable cause, supported by Oath or affirmation, and particularly describing the place to be searched, and the persons or things to be seized.

What does this protect? (*According to Findlaw*)
1. A law enforcement officer's physical apprehension or "seizure" of a person, by way of a stop or arrest; and
2. Police searches of places and items in which an individual has a legitimate expectation of privacy – his or her person, clothing, purse, luggage, vehicle, house, apartment, hotel room, and place of business, to name a few examples.

There are many devices the founders never imagined. We could equate the modern day smartphone, laptop, or tablet to the notepads of yesteryear. Any place we have an expectation of privacy is protected from search and seizure. If we don't have an expectation of privacy in our homes, on our bodies, our most intimate phone calls, or our most personal writings, then we have none.

The government in every form has been proven it can't be entrusted with the power given though technology. We must find ways to limit the risk of abuse or we shall forever find ourselves living in a panopticon.

Government Protection or Loss of Liberty?

Published on

The Teatarian

Our government has decided that they need to see our nude bodies or demand intrusive body searches. They do this all in the name of safety as we fly. There is all this extreme caution at airports, yet not one terrorist has ever been caught by a TSA agent.

The 9/11 hijackers and the so-called Christmas day bomber were not found by TSA agents despite the fact government had been alerted to the danger prior to the attacks. We know that the average terrorists are Muslim with dark complexions, and are between the ages of 17 and 34. If we know this, why do we have government personnel searching white elderly people and children? They do it in the name of being politically correct. They will pass up the opportunity to search someone fitting the profile of a terrorist and intimately search a child. They are also doing this in their war on drugs that has failed miserably.

These agents are touching children in ways parents have taught the child to fear and report. The government now wants to see our children naked in an effort to keep us safe. Do we want protection that badly? I know I don't and will refuse to fly.

Recently a concerned citizen decided to map all traffic cameras in the city. Homeland Security labeled him a potential terrorist and without a warrant, a GPS tracking device was placed on his car. He did this only to point out how often and where the government is watching people.

Today we must pass through metal detectors to visit many of our national treasures. We must be ready to submit to having our purses and bodies searched in the name of safety. The government is conditioning us to more and more surveillance. At what point do we say no and decide that safety and political correctness aren't worth the loss of our civil liberties?

Every time a terrorist has been stopped, it has been by the very citizens that are being harassed in security. There is not one single instance of these extreme government measures stopping one terrorist.

We have a government that refuses to search someone that fits the profile of a terrorist. We have a government that refuses to secure our borders and to deport those that come here illegally. We have cities giving sanctuary and aid to those that break our laws, while we are forced to give those same cities federal dollars. Yet we have strangers, who are government agents, groping our children like some child molester.

Homeland Security is promising us that these nude images they demand of us in airports are not retained or transmitted. How many times has government made such promises to find later that there had been an error and millions of bytes of personal information has gotten into the hands of nefarious types?

Tea Partiers are being labeled as terrorist, while we search children in airports. Is this the country our founders envisioned? I believe with what we are seeing from our government, especially by TSA officers, that it's they who are the real terrorists.

If you are in the hands of the TSA and decide in the middle of the search that you change your mind and choose not to fly, you are still not allowed to leave. If you interrupt one of these searches you can be fined $10,000 dollars and subject to a civil suit.

Welcome to The People's Republic of Socialist America
Former title: *Government Protection or Loss of Rights?*

Various Topics

Stand Your Ground

Published on
7/21/13 4:00 PM

The president of the United States, the head of the NAACP, and various other democrats are saying we need to remove all stand your ground laws. They tell us to prevent there being more Trayvons we must stop profiling. The left believes we shouldn't have guns with which to protect ourselves.

Let's look at how the events in Florida might have played out if Trayvon had reacted differently to the situation. Trayvon would have seen Zimmerman watching and following him. Trayvon could have run away, which would have been my option. If he was really in fear he could have called 911. If Trayvon had fled, this would have only been an obscure 911 call. Humans, when faced with an unknown situation, will follow their instincts, which are fight or flight.

In the America Obama envisions no one would have guns, or if they did exist their use would rarely be a legal. We know that crime is rampant in this country. We know that most of the crimes are done by repeat offenders. We know that criminals are often simply given a slap on the wrist. We know that police response times average about 9 minutes. I dare say that is a very low number. If you live in a rural area you know it can take far longer for an officer to respond to an emergency, especially at night when many police departments operate with reduced personnel.

Let's present this scenario. A woman lives alone ten miles out of town. She is awakened by someone breaking through a patio door. It's dark – her phone is across the room in the charger. She will have 20 seconds to make a decision. Does she go for the phone and call 911, knowing the police are at least 10 minutes or much more away. Or she has a gun under her bed. She grabs it and points it toward the bedroom door. He enters the bedroom and she fires.

In today's world there are several outcomes. The first is he is wounded and retreats. He is permanently disabled from the shooting. He sues her for millions. There are several cases where the intruder was awarded large sums of money in similar cases.

The second is she hesitates, the intruder spots the gun, and runs. He gets way, but three nights later the same thing happens again at another residence, this time the woman isn't armed. She is brutally raped and nearly dies. This is a scenario that's repeated often all over the country.

The third, she fires and kills the intruder. There is plenty of evidence to back up her story. In some parts of the country she would be charged with manslaughter, or she might be charged with the illegal possession, or use of a firearm. In too many places the potential rapist becomes the victim because by some law he wouldn't have been a rapist until he actually raped her.

As long as a criminal knows there are likely to be no consequences for their actions, they are emboldened. If that criminal knows there is a gun in the house they are less likely to commit a crime. The Aurora theater shooter traveled much farther from his home than necessary because he was looking for one that banned concealed weapons.

Let's move on to profiling. Let's start by saying there is profiling for many different reasons. Yes, blacks are often profiled because of many reasons. Just turn on the television, no matter if its the news or movies, you see blacks as the perpetrator of crime. Statistics seem to support that blacks commit more crime disproportionately to their population.

Bikers are often profiled by the way they dress and their mode of transportation. The reason for this is bikers have in the past had a reputation for being violent criminals, even if that's not true of today's bikers. Even though the large percentage of bikers are career oriented individuals, they still can evoke nervousness in a populous that knows only the tales of violent biker gangs.

Have I ever seen someone approaching in a mall parking lot and hurriedly locked my doors? You bet I have and I dare say most women have at some time. Did this occur more often with blacks approaching? I have no idea. As a human we have "vibes." This is some instinct of self preservation. We don't always know what triggers that response. I do know that I have never feared someone simply because of skin color. I live in an area where approximately 40% of the population is black. I would live in constant fear if skin color triggered the fear factor, no... there is much more.

One thing is for sure, if that person tries to enter my car or house they automatically become the enemy. If that person comes on my property uninvited and doesn't immediately try to make contact with me or someone in my family, they become the enemy. They are to be perceived as a threat.

Trayvon entered private property when he cut between houses. He should have been looked on with a wary eye. He should have been watched because that's what one does when in a "Neighborhood Watch" program. The moment Trayvon chose to give up his right to flee and turned to face Zimmerman, he became the aggressor. The moment he hit Zimmerman, he became the criminal. From that point on I say that Zimmerman had the right to use his weapon.

We often hear asked – what if Trayvon had been white and Zimmerman was black. Trayvon would still be dead. You can make Zimmerman female and the results would be the same. The aggressor would be shot.

The simple rule of thumb is violence begets violence. Legs before fist is always the best option. If Trayvon had followed those simple rules he would still be alive. The politicians have made this a gun issue. Their goal is to create an unarmed populous in the misguided belief that will end murder and other crimes. In their efforts to remove guns they are as well dividing the races. If they had labeled Zimmerman correctly as being Hispanic, that would have made this case useless for their purposes. We must all stop participating in their games and look at things honestly. Thankfully those 6 jurors looked at only the facts.

Are there really Communist?

People make fun of Conservatives, Republicans, Tea Party, and others when they speak of Communist, Marxists, and socialists. Often those on the right are said to see Communist on every corner. There is a lot of evidence to show these fears aren't unfounded, especially today when many people in political power are proud to call themselves progressive or socialist. Hillary Clinton is happy to admit she is a progressive, which is just a more acceptable term for socialist or communist.

There are beliefs of varying degrees when it comes to any group. There are those that feel some socialism or communism is a good thing. They could possibly be right, but those things would have to be done on the state level if we are going to follow the Constitution and keep the country a republic.

All organizations change or evolve over time. It's obviously clear neither the Democratic or Republican Parties are the same they were in the beginning. During the 20's and 30's progressives clearly had control of the Democratic Party. It was progressive beliefs that caused the *Great Depression*. Only in the USA did the economic depression last for so long, and only in the USA is it referred to as the *Great Depression.*

pro·gres·sive *Noun: A person advocating or implementing social reform or new, liberal ideas.*

During the John Kennedy era of the 50's and 60's the party moved somewhat away from the progressive ideology. After the *Great Depression* the term progressive was mostly stricken from the leftist vocabulary. Democrats were too happy to be called liberal, which implies freedom and liberty. During the founding days being a liberal was a good thing. Those were the people who stood for liberty and not government suppression. In some ways the Democratic Party is liberal because it often stands for individual rights. In other instances they take away individual rights. I find that both of the current political parties are very selective of the rights they choose to protect. Be assured that none of the socialist styled ideologies are for liberal causes unless it can further their agenda. Libertarians are the only ones that fight for all liberties.

Let's use gay marriage as an example. Today it is the Democratic Party that seems to support gay marriage. This is only if you look at the surface. In some areas of the country democrats support gay marriage, while in others they often support traditional marriage laws, the same as many republicans. If the Democratic Party was truly for gay marriage they would have legalized it in 2008 when they had control of the House, Senate, and White House.

If the Democratic Party was truly liberal it would work to remove marriage from government control. A true liberal or libertarian believes that government has no business deciding with whom someone lives. When asked, a Democrat will tell you government needs to control marriage because of taxes. We then must have to ask, why would someone who stands for liberty wish to tax someone differently simply because they are married or have children?

All we hear from the left is equality, except they only want it on their terms. By taxing married couples less than individuals you create an inequality. They want people who work hard and earn more money to pay a higher percentage of taxes than their fellow Americans. The left demands you show your identification to buy certain medicines, while crying it is wrong to ask for the same ID while voting. I compare progressivism and socialism to Robin Hood. Take from the rich and give to the poor.

Now that we know what isn't a Communist. To understand something you must first know what it is. Communist is derived from the world *commune*. This is a society where everyone works for the common good. All the farmers would deliver their goods to a distribution point and elders selected by the people or through linage would divide the crops to people by need. A farmer who produced twice as many crops would receive the same amount of food as the one who produced much less. Both farmers have a wife and four children so they are equal in need.

If a country was to be totally communist all goods and income would be sent to the government where it would be divided among the population by need. This is nearly an impossible task in large modern countries. In today's world communism is often modulated with socialism and capitalism.

China is a good example of this mix. Today communism in China is often referred to as state capitalism. Many in the USA who belief capitalism alone is evil, believe state capitalism is the direction in which this country should move. What these people fail to mention is that China is doomed to fail.

China's economy is based on a false currency. The government makes sure that the Yuan is kept far below its natural value. The USA itself has come to depend on the Chinese currency to curb its own inflation. This is why China hasn't been pressured to fairly value its currency. If China wasn't a communist nation the currency value would be controlled by the market. In essence, the USA moving to the Federal Reserve System is doing much the same thing. Through use of the Federal Reserve the US government manipulates the value of the dollar.

In the end, most of the Chinese people are very poor and do not receive the benefits of the Chinese booming export business. As with all socialist and Communist countries, the poor tend to stay poor, while in a in a free market society the poor can, and do, become millionaires, or at least achieve middle-class status.

I need to go back and explain why China is doomed to fail. We have to only look at American history to understand why. In the 70's manufacturing began to desert the northern states where unions had driven up labor cost and fled to the south where labor was cheap and unions were rare. In time wages began to rise in the south, while they remained low in Mexico and parts of South American. Trade agreements with China became permanent, where in the past each year they were reviewed before renewal. Those southern jobs began to move south of the border and then to China. At the time of this writing the USA has over 8% unemployment while Mexico's is just over 5%.

As long as China can force people to work for near nothing, then the country will flourish. History tells us that eventually the Chinese worker will demand more and more wages. At some point there will be some other country that will have cheaper labor. Japan is a good example of this shift. Japan survived only by entering the technology market. The USA is doing much the same.

Currently the USA is leaving its borders porous to allow cheap labor to enter from semi-socialist Mexico where many live in poverty. By importing illegal labor the USA is able to save some of its manufacturing.

Now that we know what a communist is, we can now look at how the communist, socialist, progressives, and the

Democratic Party interact. On October 2ⁿᵈ, 2010 democrats, unions, and Communist Party gathered at the National Mall in Washington DC.

The American Dream

The left and right have a different perspective of the American Dream. On the right we believe that anyone can work hard and become wealthy. We believe that a person has the right to be as rich or as poor as they desire. There are people born everyday who are happy doing menial jobs with no responsibility.

The left seems to believe that everyone needs a college education, or at least some trade school training. The favorite slogans of the left are, "fair share" or "Share the wealth." This is why the US has the progressive tax structure where one is taxed differently according to income and status in society. The simple act of getting married can lower your taxes. Earning one dollar over a government set figure can increase your taxes dramatically. I remember one year I received my usual annual cost of living raise, which was approximately 35 cents an hour. That increase caused me to bring home one dollar less each week simply because I was put in a higher tax bracket.

All societies need janitors, trash collectors, and people to sweep the floor. In the past those jobs were reserved for the uneducated. In today's "push for college" society, labor has to be imported from Latin American countries to do those menial jobs.

One night I got into a debate with a far left guy who described himself as an anarchist or a libertarian. He sadly had no idea that he was a Communist. This guy believed a janitor should make the same wages as a doctor. He figured a doctor should be educated for free and that would make it fair that they would earn the same wages. It didn't seem to matter that it took far more work to become a doctor. He thought a person becomes a doctor by choice and shouldn't earn more for the increased responsibility.

Many on the left can't see the American dream isn't just to become wealthy. The American dream is the right to do the work they enjoy. There are cases where a person is an excellent auto mechanic, for example, and would love to repair cars in his backyard garage for extra income. He can't do this because of zoning and insurance requirements.

In Coralville, Iowa police shut down 4-year-old Abigail Krstinger's lemonade stand after it had been up for half an hour. They were informed it would cost $400 dollars for the proper permits. The children were selling cups of lemonade for 25 cents and had made no more than $5.00.

This is an extreme, but if the person wants to work on cars in his backyard, and all the customers are aware that he isn't a licensed mechanic, and there are no neighbor complaints, what is the problem?

In most rural areas it's legal to grow crops and then set up a roadside stand in which to sell them to passing motorist. If this happened in suburban areas they would be arrested. In the south it's common for people to make weekly trips to the farmer's market where they buy produce to sell in these roadside stands. This is the American dream, the entrepreneurial freedom that built American. Those children who were denied lemonade stands will lose the entrepreneurial spirit.

Van Jones said to the progressive Netroots conference:

So let me make sure you understand what I mean when I say killing the American Dream. I'm not talking killing American Fantasy, okay?

The American Fantasy: Everybody's going to be rich, you buy a lot of things, you'll be happy. No, that's the American Fantasy, which has led to an American

T. L. Crain

Nightmare. That needs to go, that needs to go, that needs to go… we don't believe in that, we don't believe in that at all. I'm talking about something much, much deeper than that, something that we had in this country before the commercializers turned it into something else: The American Dream, which is simply the idea that hard work should pay in our country, that you should be able to get up in the morning in America, and if you're willing to and able to work, walk out your front door, go to a dignified job, put in a good day's work, and come back home with a paycheck and can feed your family with it and give your children a better life: That's the American Dream.

The left is always talking about how they love everyone and believe all people are equal. They claim to embrace all lifestyles, yet they believe if you dig ditches or clean bathrooms you don't have a dignified job. A person can do any job with dignity. A society of any form has nasty jobs. If anyone has ever watched the Discovery Channel program *Dirty Jobs* they will see there are many nasty jobs to be done. Are any of these jobs not dignified?

The object of working is to buy things to make our lives more comfortable and enjoyable. If not for these things, then why work? Many on the left believe people need only the basic items in life. During the Reagan administration the term "Trickle-down economics" became popular. This was the leftist term for "supply-side economics." This is where you lower taxes and reduce regulations on businesses so they can expand and hire more people. The economic fact is that when the employer makes more profit some will go to the employees. Socialism is said to be "trickle-up poverty." Because of government regulation and taxation, the American middle class might become extinct. Unless John Doe can repair cars in his backyard we will have more and more poverty. After being laid off, John Doe was forced to go on unemployment compensation where he must beg the government for money on which to feed his family. If there is no government approved job by the end of that payment period he will be forced to beg for welfare.

The unemployment numbers we so often see and hear on the news are based on how many people are drawing unemployment compensation. Once those checks stop coming in they are no longer counted as unemployed. People like me are not thought to be unemployed. The chart shows the real numbers and they are staggering. In 2011 and 2012 almost a fifth of potential workers were unemployed. All of this is happening while the left works hard to save the jobs of those who entered the country illegally, and illegally hold jobs.

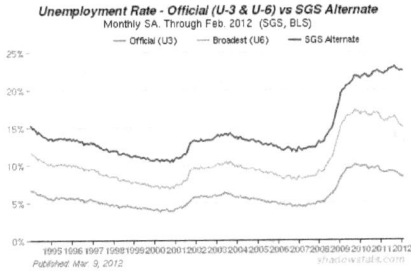

Unemployment Rate - Official (U-3 & U-6) vs SGS Alternate
Monthly SA. Through Feb. 2012 (SGS, BLS)

The true American dream of being as rich as you desire is the only thing that will solve unemployment woes. If a person is willing to do the job for what the employer is willing to pay, then the job is dignified. Undignified jobs are those illegal immigrants hold while working below market standard wages for fear of being reported to immigration agencies.

Federal Blackmail

The National Maximum Speed Limit of 55 M.P.H. was created in 1974 when Richard Nixon signed the Emergency Energy Highway Conservation Act. This came about because of the OPEC oil embargo that caused rationing and long gas lines in the 70's. It was decided that with lower speed limits, even on interstate highways, the country could save gas. There were claims the reduced speed limit saved 167,000 barrels of oil a day.

If this saved gas or not, that is not the problem, it's how the federal government chose to enforce these mandatory speed limits. Regulating speeds limits was clearly a power afforded to the states. The only way the federal government could force states to change speed limits was to withhold federal funds. This was never seriously challenged in the courts so government now had a new way to circumvent the Constitution. This law was overturned in 1995.

The federal government uses the same tactic to control the school system. Nowhere in the Constitution is education mentioned. Since the document didn't give any power to the federal government over education, then that power is reserved for the states.

History of the Department of Education

The original Department of Education was created in 1867 to collect information on schools and teaching that would help the States establish effective school systems. While the agency's name and location within the Executive Branch have changed over the past 130 years, this early emphasis on getting information on what works in education to teachers and education policymakers continues down to the present day.

Passage of the Second Morrill Act in 1890 gave the then-named Office of Education responsibility for administering support for the original system of land-grant colleges and universities. Vocational education became the next major area of Federal aid to schools, with the 1917 Smith-Hughes Act and the 1946 George-Barden Act focusing on agricultural, industrial, and home economics training for high school students.

World War II led to a significant expansion of Federal support for education. The Lanham Act in 1941 and the

Impact Aid laws of 1950 eased the burden on communities affected by the presence of military and other Federal installations by making payments to school districts. And in 1944, the "GI Bill" authorized post-secondary education assistance that would ultimately send nearly 8 million World War II veterans to college.

The Cold War stimulated the first example of comprehensive Federal education legislation, when in 1958 Congress passed the National Defense Education Act (NDEA) in response to the Soviet launch of Sputnik. To help ensure that highly trained individuals would be available to help America compete with the Soviet Union in scientific and technical fields, the NDEA included support for loans to college students, the improvement of science, mathematics, and foreign language instruction in elementary and secondary schools, graduate fellowships, foreign language and area studies, and vocational-technical training.

The anti-poverty and civil rights laws of the 1960s and 1970s brought about a dramatic emergence of the Department's equal access mission. The passage of laws such as Title VI of the Civil Rights Act of 1964, Title IX of the Education Amendments of 1972, and Section 504 of the Rehabilitation Act of 1973 which prohibited discrimination based on race, sex, and disability, respectively made civil rights enforcement a fundamental and long-lasting focus of the Department of Education. In 1965, the Elementary and Secondary Education Act launched a comprehensive set of programs, including the Title I program of Federal aid to disadvantaged children to address the problems of poor urban and rural areas. And in that same year, the Higher Education Act authorized assistance for post-secondary education, including financial aid programs for needy college students.

In 1980, Congress established the Department of Education as a Cabinet level agency. Today, Education Department operates programs that touch on every area and level of education. The Department's elementary and secondary programs annually serve nearly 14,000 school districts and some 56 million students attending roughly 99,000 public schools and 34,000 private schools. Department programs also provide grant, loan, and work-study assistance to more than 15 million post secondary students. (*Source www2.ed.gov*)

Because the federal government has no legal standing over state education, they use the same blackmail tactics as they did enforcing the 55 mph speed limit. The federal government first collects taxes and then divides them to the states only if they follow the federally mandated regulations. The Teatarian believes education is best left to states and communities. The USA is continuously falling in education ranking among industrialized nations. It's clear the federal government is failing. More than half the people polled believe education spending should be increased. Spending has gone from 1% GDP in 1900 to 6% GDP in 2012. I give the federal government a failing grade for its interference in education

The Main Stream Media

Some like to believe the ideological right is paranoid when it comes to the media. To answer this I'd like to tell the story of how I came to be whom I am ideologically, which is libertarian. This goes back to my teen years when I first began to really pay attention to the news on television. This was in the 60's so there were only 3 or 4 television stations before PBS came along.

The thing I began to notice over time was that no matter the station, the news was essentially the same. As years passed and television stations doubled, I noticed the same thing. They often repeated the same words. Back then I was very ideologically liberal and often agreed with much they said. I guess people assumed that no one on radio, television, or the newspaper would deliberately lie. Maybe the lies weren't deliberate and they had been manipulated by their sources.

As a science and science fiction buff I loved reading about unidentified flying saucers (UFOs) and the Roswell incident. First let me say, I'm not talking about whether UFOs are real or not, but how the government handled the event at Roswell and sightings of experimental military aircraft. The government turned the sightings into a joke and declared those who saw things a little off in the head. The government does the same thing today, but not only with sightings of secret aircraft, but with anything about which they don't want the public pressuring them. I have coined this government manipulation the UFO syndrome.

The UFO syndrome is a common tactic of the left and the main stream media. Even the president stands before the press and laughs when asked question to which he doesn't want to reply.

I need to point out the media, for the most part, isn't corrupt, it's just those who are attracted to that field tend to be left oriented. Some suggest it's the journalism schools that point them left. We do know that Iranian president, Mahmoud Ahmadinejad, was mostly given respect while speaking at Columbia University. Ann Coulter was almost hit with a pie, while other Conservatives were unable to complete their speech.

Today we have dozens of news channels and they all tell you the same stories in almost the same words. I see that much of the news comes from the Associated Press and all the other news sources simply reprint or read the wire service script. Maybe the problem with journalism today is that they are just lazy.

Political correctness is another reason the media is like it is today. They don't want to offend any viewers because in the end it's a business. The more viewers they have the more they can charge for commercials. The left believes PBS and NPR is the solution. On the surface commercial free news sounds like it would be the answer, except for the fact that the nonprofit sources tend to be more biased than the rest.

Last year black journalist Juan Williams was fired from PBS for saying that he sometimes got nervous when flying with Muslims in traditional garb. I'm sure he was expressing feelings that many have. Williams said about his firing on the O'Reilly Factor, "I don't fit in their box. I'm not a predictable, black liberal." He also stated he believes he was fired because, "I appear on Fox,"

NPR CEO Vivian Schiller later ordered news staffers not to attend John Stewart's political rally in Washington DC. This was the right decision by Schiller, but we must be concerned that it was such a problem the CEO had to step in and make the mandate.

The latest event was when Georgetown law student, Sandra Fluke, appeared before a congressional committee to protest the Jesuit university's policy of not paying for birth control. Rush Limbaugh said on his program that by Fluke wanting the university to pay for contraceptives she in a sense wanted someone to pay her to have sex, which "makes her a slut."

A few days later Rush apologized and then later on his radio show said, "You never descend to the level of your opponent or they win, that was my error last week," Limbaugh added, "But the apology was heart-felt. The apology was sincere."

He did take the diatribe about Fluke too far and for that he was attacked by almost every major news source. Some have even gone to the FCC in order to have the entertainer removed from radio. Attacks on Limbaugh and calls for his show to be removed are regular events. The left seems to think free speech is precious only when it's their own.

The onslaught of Rush brought reminders of Bill Maher

calling Sara Palin a "cunt" and even making jokes about her autistic child. And then Maher said, "Bristol Palin has to admit that the reason she f**ked Levi over and over until a baby fell out is because she liked it." He further quipped that the book's working title was "Whoops, there's a d**k in me."

The media and the left in general excused Maher by stating that he was a comedian and had the right to say anything he wanted. Even women's groups never came to Bristol's defense. The president took the time to call Sandra Fluke and apologize for what Rush said, but he offered no sympathy for Bristol, Sara, or Michelle Bachmann who as well has had vile things said about her. The media has clearly showed bias against Conservative females.

The book *Rules for Radicals* by Saul D. Alinsky, who is said to be the first community organizer, is held in high esteem by those on the left. They use his book as a guideline for advancing the leftist agenda. Alinsky believed that a movement must fan hostilities in order to get people to participate.

Could the media be complicit in fanning hostilities for this purpose? The races became even more divided when we heard the headlines "White Watch Captain guns down candy eating African-American teen." This story sounds cut and dry until you begin to dig into this story. At this point it's hard to say if deadly force was justified since the shooter, George Zimmerman, had injuries to the front and back of his head. He is claiming self defense. There are witnesses that tell us Zimmerman was the one who was attacked. For the moment this isn't important since I am discussing the media.

NBC has been caught playing an edited version of the 911 audio.

Zimmerman: This guy looks like he's up to no good. He looks black.

185

And here is how it actually occurred:

> *Zimmerman: This guy looks like he's up to no good. Or he's on drugs or something. It's raining and he's just walking around, looking about.*

> *Dispatcher: OK, and this guy — is he black, white or Hispanic?*

> *Zimmerman: He looks black.*

While NBC denies this was intentional, we can only be skeptical. If anyone has ever watched MSNBC, the network's political bias is obvious. Obama and the Democrats, along with help from the media, work to divide the country by class and race. Because this is deliberate, you can't hear or read something from a media source and declare it true. You can't say it's the truth because you hear all the stations repeating the same thing. To find the truth we have to often go outside what is considered the *main stream media*.

Since the writing of this piece Zimmerman filed a lawsuit against NBC. In early July, 2014 that lawsuit was dismissed. The judge ruled that Zimmerman was a public figure that gave weight to NBC, which allowed them leniency in their reporting.

Who do we trust if not the media?

This is a hard question to answer. The Teatarian will look for sources they feel can be trusted. I personally feel, that most often, Rush Limbaugh, Mark Levin, Neil Boortz, and local talk hosts on WBT radio in Charlotte, N.C. are some of the most reliable. I often source Walter E. Williams and he is surely one of my most trusted sources. For as long as I can remember, John Stossel is someone I have held in high esteem. He no doubt had a lot to do with who I am today politically. More recently there are those like Megyn Kelly of Fox News. I have also watched Glenn Beck evolve over the years to someone who is more libertarian. There is no one with whom I agree one hundred percent, but some garner more trust than others. We must always question what we see and hear.

The Teatarian will often evoke the Constitution, so for that reason Mark Levin has to be a very important source. He is founder and CEO of Landmark Legal, which has written many legal briefs for a variety of constitutional causes.

Beginning in 1981, Levin served as adviser to several members of President Ronald Reagan's cabinet, eventually becoming Associate Director of Presidential Personnel and ultimately Chief of Staff to Attorney General Edwin Meese; Levin also served as Deputy Assistant Secretary for Elementary and Secondary Education at the U.S. Department of Education, and Deputy Solicitor of the U.S. Department of the Interior.

Too often we have to wonder if one of our trusted sources is in the business simply to make money. Even though I do often turn to Glenn Beck for information, I have sometimes worried if he wasn't in this for the money. He does seem to be an honorable man. Mark Levin offers no paid membership for his website. The archives of all his radio shows are free. That makes me think he is less into this for the money.

No matter in whom you place trust, that trust must always be tinged with a healthy dose of skepticism. We must listen to those with a different side of the story. Often we hear that the truth lies somewhere in the middle. I don't believe that to be the case when you find people with whom you can place your trust.

Whenever we see and hear polling numbers, or the results of some study, we have only to wait and there will be some poll or study that tells a different story. Often it takes time for the truth to develop. We can only hope it doesn't take so long that we can't make informed decisions at the polling booth. Trust no one implicitly.

Medicinal Marijuana

The Teatarian is completely libertarian when it comes to drugs, while the Tea Party movement is divided among conservatives and libertarians. I would say most conservatives are not for the legalization of marijuana in any form, but would be agreeable to decriminalization. Most feel prisons are costly and there are too many nonviolent offenders being incarcerated.

I would like to speak more about my libertarian view of the subject. Let's first look at how laws against marijuana first came about. Hemp at the time was the most popular source of marijuana. Hemp was used for making rope. In the 60's a common term for smoking marijuana was "smoking rope."

For two years Congress secretly deliberated until if finally passed the Marijuana Tax Stamp Act of 1937. The first serious regulation of marijuana was 1906 in Washington DC. By 1930, sixteen states had banned the use of marijuana except for medicinal purposes.

The push to ban cocaine and opium (and later marijuana) at the federal level ran into a serious obstacle – the Tenth Amendment to the United States Constitution, which stated powers not delegated to the federal government through the Constitution were reserved for the states. The federal government would not be denied and used taxes and regulation to control the use of marijuana, as well as other drugs. In 1969 the Marijuana Tax Stamp Act of 1937 was found to be unconstitutional. Once again the federal government refused to be denied power and the U.S. Congress responded by passing The Controlled Substances Act in 1970, citing "interstate commerce" as the basis for its authority. The U.S. Supreme Court recognized the so-called "commerce clause" to uphold a series of laws that effectively gutted the Tenth Amendment's reservation of powers for the states and to the people. The commerce clause has been used to literally gut the Constitution.

This leads us to the current time when states are passing medicinal marijuana laws. For the most part, the DEA hasn't harassed these sellers. I find we have a federal government that is afraid to make hard decisions in order to clarify the laws. Just the label "medicinal marijuana" indicates this is a medicine of some fashion. Most state laws say that a patient must have a prescription from a doctor in order to obtain the marijuana. If this is a medicine and needs a doctor's recommendation to use and obtain medicinal marijuana, then shouldn't it come under FDA regulations? Below is what the Food and Drug Administration says it doesn't regulate.

What FDA Does Not Regulate

FDA's responsibilities are closely related to those of several other government agencies. Often frustrating and confusing for consumers is determining the appropriate regulatory agency to contact. The following contact information is for government agencies that have functions related to that of FDA. (Contact information is given for agency headquarters offices, which are located in the Washington, D.C., area. Local offices, listed in the phone book under U.S. Government, may be available to provide assistance as well.)

Yes this is very vague so let's see if we can find some better clarification.

Drugs of Abuse

Illegal drugs with no approved medical use--such as heroin and marijuana—are under the jurisdiction of the Drug Enforcement Administration. FDA assists DEA in deciding how stringent DEA controls should be on drugs that are medically accepted, but that have a strong potential for abuse. DEA establishes limits on the amount of these prescription drugs that are permitted to be manufactured each year. Inquiries regarding DEA activities may be sent to the Drug Enforcement Administration, U.S. Department of Justice, Washington, DC 20537; telephone (202)   307-1000.

Are you more confused yet? The above is information from the current FDA website. It says that marijuana has no medicinal value. The psychoactive compound in marijuana is delta-9-tetrahydrocannabinol, commonly referred to as THC. Although cannabis and any products obtained from the plant are classified as Schedule I substances, some products derived from or related to marijuana can be legally obtained by prescription in the U.S. or Canada. The synthetic form is available as *Dronabinol (Marinol) and abilone (Cesamet)*. Those are classified as schedule III drugs.

It's clear to see there is a lot of confusion when it comes to laws concerning marijuana, especially the medicinal type. I ask that the federal government provide consistency in laws and regulations, as well as accepting the limits placed upon it by the Constitution. If marijuana is a medicine then it should be controlled by the FDA. If it is a food supplement, then it should be sold as such. It is clearly a drug the federal government has deemed bad in its natural state, while in the synthetic form it is described as a medicine, which falls under the control of the FDA.

The Commerce Clause in the Constitution clearly states it is to regulate commerce between the states. The founders wanted to insure that states would trade freely with one another. According to the Constitution if a person wanted to grow marijuana to use for their own purposes it wouldn't fall under the commerce clause. The laws upheld by the Supreme Court of the USA, which are based on the commerce clause, shouldn't apply unless there was interstate commerce.

The 10th Amendment Nullification Movement

"If the federal government has the exclusive right to judge the extent of its own powers, warned the Kentucky and Virginia resolutions' authors (Thomas Jefferson and James Madison, respectively), it will continue to grow – regardless of elections, the separation of powers, and other much-touted limits on government power."–**Thomas E. Woods**

The Energy Independence and Security Act of 2007 spells the end to household use of incandescent light bulbs 100 watts and below. Light bulbs from 40 watts through 100 watts must be 25% more efficient by the following dates: The beginning of 2012 for 100 watt bulbs – The beginning of 2013 for 75 watt bulbs – The beginning of 2014 for 40 and 60 watt bulbs. I feel this is an abuse of federal powers. Tea Party minded states are seeking to retake power that should be reserved for the states. South Carolina passed the South Carolina, Ayn Rand and the Incandescent Light Bulb Freedom Act. This law states that any incandescent manufactured and sold within state borders did not have to comply with the federal law that effectively banned most incandescent light bulbs.

Of course it's going to take time to see if the justice department will challenge the law. Laws such as this one are a direct challenge to the federal government in hopes of restoring the republic and state powers.

This goes much farther than simple light bulbs. The left in general hates firearms of any fashion and often pass laws either banning them or placing severe restrictions on ownership. There is a real fear that if the leftist Democratic Party ever gets total power they may ban guns.

Amendment II
A well regulated Militia, being necessary to the security of a free state, the right of the people to keep and bear Arms, shall not be infringed.

The left tries to tell us the 2nd Amendment only allows people to form a militia. The Teatarin believes the meaning is quite clear and it intended for citizens of states to be armed. The founders weren't worried as much about foreign invaders as the time could arrive when the state might have to defend itself from the federal government. Those worries were later proven true after the Confederate States of America was attacked by the U.S government.

The Firearms Freedom Act (FFA) is sweeping the Nation, which was originally introduced and passed in Montana. This law states that any firearms made and retained in-state are beyond the authority of Congress under its constitutional power to regulate commerce among the states.

Montana, Wyoming, Idaho, South Dakota, Utah, Arizona, and Tennessee have also passed the FFA. Twenty-one states have introduced legislation, including South Carolina. Other states intend to pass some form of legislation that does the same thing.

Amendment X

The powers not delegated to the United States by the Constitution, nor prohibited by it to the States, are reserved to the States respectively, or to the people.

Thomas Jefferson first introduced nullification in his draft of the Kentucky Resolutions of 1798. In the Virginia Resolutions of 1798, James Madison said, "The states are duty bound to resist when the federal government violated the Constitution."

Nullification isn't just something to read about in the history books. Two dozen American states nullified the Real ID Act of 2005. States passing medicinal marijuana laws are effectively nullification. The federal government has sat nervously by and has rarely raided the shops that sell the medicinal marijuana. If the United States is to be preserved as the founders intended then states must use every tool at their disposal, which are many.

Tobacco

I have talked about government over regulation of drugs. The most used drug in society, next to alcohol and caffeine, is tobacco. Before I begin, I must confess to being a former smoker – yes we are the worst kind. I stopped smoking on January 6th, 2000. I personally wish everyone in the world would quit smoking, but I will defend their right to smoke. I could go on about the dangers of smoking, but won't.

Let's talk about the progressive agenda and smoking. Tobacco in almost every form is a legal product to buy and sell as long as you are over 18 years of age. Tobacco is one of the most taxed products in the USA.

Excise Tax Per Pack (USD)	State/Territory
0.425	Alabama
2.00	Alaska
2.00	Arizona
1.15	Arkansas

0.87	California
0.84	Colorado
3.40	Connecticut
1.60	Delaware
1.339	Florida
0.37	Georgia
3.20	Hawaii
0.57	Idaho
0.98	Illinois
0.995	Indiana
1.36	Iowa
0.79	Kansas
0.60	Kentucky
0.36	Louisiana
2.00	Maine
2.00	Maryland
2.51	Massachusetts
2.00	Michigan
1.60	Minnesota
0.68	Mississippi
0.17	Missouri
1.70	Montana
0.64	Nebraska
0.80	Nevada
1.68	New Hampshire
2.70	New Jersey
1.66	New Mexico
4.35	New York
0.45	North Carolina
0.44	North Dakota
1.25	Ohio
1.03	Oklahoma
1.18	Oregon
1.60	Pennsylvania
3.46	Rhode Island

0.57	South Carolina
1.53	South Dakota
0.62	Tennessee
1.41	Texas
1.70	Utah
2.62	Vermont
0.30	Virginia
3.025	Washington
0.55	West Virginia
2.52	Wisconsin
0.60	Wyoming
2.50	Dist. of Columbia
1.75	Northern Marianas Islands
2.23	Puerto Rico
3.00	Guam
2.50	American Samoa

There is one thing progressives love more than control, and that's taxes. Only through taxes can they manage their social programs. Tobacco taxes and lotteries have often been called a tax on the poor and middle class, the groups progressives claim to protect.

Tobacco, in some cases, is as dangerous as the medical community proposes. The EPA has even gotten involved when it comes to secondhand smoking. Secondhand smoking is the reason that governments, local and federal, have passed smoking bans in most public buildings, even though many of these bans extend to outside areas. Some local governments have extended smoking bans to city owned property. If the intention was to protect nonsmokers then the indoor bans would be enough.

Those of us that study progressives find that they do want to protect people from the harmful effects of smoking, but they also want to collect taxes and control the masses. The progressives have manage to raise taxes in hopes of making tobacco products less desirable, while at the same time using bans to control people.

Smoking laws are a good example of *creep*. Remember, this is where progressives get the people used to the idea of a law or regulation and then slowly increase its power. Progressives know that Americans would have revolted against a tobacco ban. Instead of a direct ban they began with eliminating television cigarette advertising. In 2012 the federal government spent $53 million on an ad campaign that shows severely disfigured people.

In many places you can't light up on a windy beach, the excuse is that smokers litter the beaches with cigarette butts that harm the environment. There are many things taken on beaches that would be just as harmful. These laws are clearly progressive prohibition campaigns.

If the government truly believed tobacco to be as bad as laws portray, and cared as much for people as they say, then tobacco would become an illegal drug. Former Chief of Staff Rahm Emanuel said, "Never let a disaster go to waste," as crude oil spilled into the Gulf of Mexico.

Why hate green energy?

Green energy is a term tossed around by the leftist. Some of the left have been caught on video speaking to their groups on how they plan to use environmentalism to further communism in the USA. Van Jones, the former green jobs czar, was a self professed communist in the 90's. He was arrested during the violence that followed after the Rodney King beating.

> Jones said, "I met all these young radical people of color – I mean really radical, communists and anarchists. And it was like, 'This is what I need to be a part of,'" he said in a

2005 interview with the East Bay Express. Jones told the newspaper he stayed in San Francisco, and for the next 10 years worked with a lot of the people he met in jail. Months after the King verdict came down, Jones said; "I was a communist."

This is important because Jones is deeply involved in the green movement. Environmentalism is a wonderful cause. Like everything else, moderation is always the best policy. No one wants polluted waters or a repeat of the chemical dumping of the 50's and 60's. The Comprehensive Environmental Response Compensation and Liability Act (CERCLA or Superfund) was signed into law on December 11, 1980 and was created to address the cleanup of the worst abandoned dump sites. At their 30th anniversary the EPA reported 1.3 million acres of land had been cleared and returned to productive use. No one wants a repeat.

Much of today's environmentalism is based on global warming, which after the warming trend stopped, was relabeled to climate change. Billions have been spent worldwide on climate change in the form of climate science or in subsidies to green energy firms. Obama was elected to office on the pretense of creating green jobs as millions of Americans lost theirs. By the end of his 4th term those jobs had failed to materialize.

Here is one reason why those jobs never materialized. East Coast Ethanol, LLC recently announced plans to build 110 million gallon per year ethanol plant in Chester, S.C., Seaboard, N.C., Jesup, Ga. and Campbellton, Fla, making the company the largest supplier of ethanol in the Southeast and the sixth largest in the U.S. The Chester plant was never built for a variety of reasons. Residents were disheartened when they learned the plant would likely close after ten years once federal grants expired from which the plant would operate. Currently ethanol cannot compete with fossil fuels.

The Energy Independence and Security Act of 2007 creates

an impossible goal of producing 36 billion gallons of renewable fuels, including 17 billion gallons of corn ethanol by 2022. Achieving this will require approximately 83 million acres — almost 90% of the current corn production in the entire United States. Already the forced demand for ethanol has driven up corn prices to the point that some fear those in repressed countries may face starvation.

Ethanol is not pollution free. It takes tractors to plow the fields and harvest the crops. The corn must be fertilized with nitrogen fertilizer, which is made indirectly from natural gas. Then heat must be applied to the distillery, which is likely to come from natural gas as well.

There is a hidden problem with ethanol. There are thousands of miles of pipelines by which diesel fuel, gasoline, and other oils are delivered to different regions. Sometimes a pipeline will hold many types of oil at the same time. Ethanol cannot be transmitted in those pipelines. Gasoline is piped as usual and the ethanol is trucked to the destination where it is then mixed with gasoline. In order for our cars to burn that ethanol, thousands of gallons of diesel fuel has been burned.

Another large hype is directed toward hydrogen as a potential fuel for our cars. There are some huge problems with hydrogen as a fuel. The biggest is that it's not found anywhere on the planet in its natural state. It takes energy to separate hydrogen from other molecules. Many see the ocean as a large pool of hydrogen, which is correct. Water is H_2O, 2 atoms of hydrogen and 1 oxygen atom. This would be the perfect fuel if you are worried about carbon release while burning. The problem lies in the fact that it takes more energy to release the hydrogen than you get from the hydrogen itself. There are other materials from which hydrogen is easier to obtain. Almost all hydrogen used by NASA comes from natural gas. It makes far more sense to burn ethanol (C_2H_5OH) which contains 6 hydrogen atoms and only 2 carbon atoms. What makes even more sense is to run cars on natural gas. The refined natural gas that reaches our homes is CH_4. That is only 1 carbon atom and 4 hydrogen atoms. The country already has the delivery system in place.

The USA is said to be the Saudi Arabia of natural gas and more reserves are being discovered each day. There is an estimated 20 trillion cubic feet of natural gas. As technology advances the recoverable reserves increase dramatically. And this brings us to why the Tea Party fights against the policies of the Democratic Party and the left in general. The green movement actually pushes for the use of natural gas, while at the same time fighting the drilling of wells needed to produce the gas.

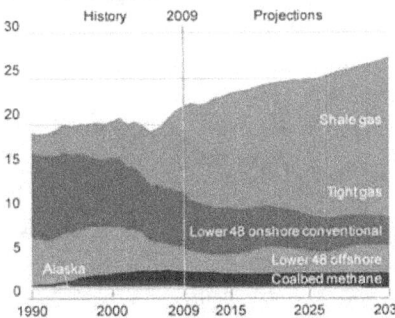

Figure 2. U.S. natural gas production, 1990-2035 (trillion cubic feet per year)

The EPA will put into effect new regulations on fracking and some say this will dramatically increase the price of natural gas. Bloomberg reports that 65% of the people polled want more regulations on fracking. Could it be the people are not properly informed? We do know democrats have an anti-drilling and an anti-oil mentality, which the main stream media helps perpetuate.

Solar photo voltaic panels could be described as free energy, at least during the daylight hours. There are many wonderful uses of solar panels. The one problem is they are not likely to come down in price anytime soon. They also lose efficiency in time. They are not something you buy once and never have to replace, but they do have a long lifespan. For myself, price is the largest problem. Right now the solar panel market is thriving because of government subsidies. That is the problem with the green market in general; they need subsidies to compete with current technologies. New nuclear power plants expect to produce electricity at 14 cents per KWH, while solar offers the same rate, except solar is government subsidized.

Today most solar PV panels are made in China. All nuclear plants are built in the USA. Do we want to trade jobs for solar? I doubt those looking for work would choose solar panels. I am all for alternative energy, I just want to let the market develop naturally. Once these technologies are fully developed and able to stand on their own merit then we can embrace them. Until that happens we need to encourage development, but rely on known technology. A thriving economy needs one thing, cheap energy. Right now the USA is holding back drilling permits while China drills off the coast of Cuba and Russia punches into the arctic. I want a common sense approach to energy.

We cannot let the unproven event of anthropogenic global warming drive the country's energy policies. The left wants us to believe there is a consensus among scientists when it comes to climate change. If this was the truth then the debate wouldn't be going at full speed. People like Al Gore, who stood to make millions off the carbon trading market, said the debate is over.

Many scientists live off grants, both government and public. If the federal government is willing to give out billions of dollars to confirm global warming, you can be sure their results will show the expected numbers. By now we all know about the hockey puck graph used to depict global warming. Everyone doesn't know the graph stops short and doesn't show the leveling of temperatures.

The left tells us over and over that drilling won't lower the price at the pump. Then they turn around and release portions of the strategic oil reserve in order to lower prices at the gasoline pump. Oil is like any other commodity, and it is traded on the commodities and futures market. If supply outpaces the demand, prices will be low. The world is using oil at record paces and to maintain a low cost, supply must be increased. The Chinese, Russians, and Canadians are well aware of this fact. While the rest of the world is working to increase oil supplies, the left in the USA is turning to government subsidized wind mills which are often built and operated by Portuguese corporations.,

2013 EPA RFS – The road to starvation

Published on
9/12/13 10:51 AM

The EPA has finished finalizing the 2013 Renewable Fuel Standards(RFS). The biggest of those changes is to increase Ethanol content in gasoline. The current standard requires all gasoline to have at least 10% Ethanol. The new standard will raise this to 15%, and will now also include diesels.

Under the Energy Independence and Security Act (EISA) of 2007, the RFS program was expanded in several key ways:

1. EISA expanded the RFS program to include diesel, in addition to gasoline;
2. EISA increased the volume of renewable fuel required to be blended into transportation fuel from 9 billion gallons in 2008 to 36 billion gallons by 2022;
3. EISA established new categories of renewable fuel, and set separate volume requirements for each one.
4. EISA required EPA to apply life-cycle greenhouse gas performance threshold standards to ensure that each category of renewable fuel emits fewer greenhouse gases than the petroleum fuel it replaces.

The source for most of this Ethanol is soybean and corn –

two main staples of our food supply. Each of those can be found in many of the processed foods we eat. Because of the USA's abundance of open, accessible fertile lands we produce much of the world's supply of food.

The USA has only so much workable farm land. More land can be cleared for farming, but then we run into increased deforestation. The country must maintain a balance between forest lands, natural preserves, and farming.

These standards also increase the market value of corn and soybean. For this reason many farmers abandon other crops and pasture lands to grow more valuable products. Because food is a global market, this effects prices around the world. Many people who were living on the edge will be pushed off the cliff into malnutrition.

We are expected to experience the following annual price increases:
3. Beef 7.5%
4. Chicken 7.7%
5. Pork 15%
6. Eggs 11.2%
7. Potatoes 13%
8. Corn products *26%*

Since 2005 food prices have increased 25% while the rate of inflation was only 16%. Add this on top of inflation created by Quantitative Easing(electronic creation of US dollars) and the consequences get even more dire for families around the world.

The sad part, this is all done in the name of global warming when all reputable scientists are predicting cooling – possibly a mini ice age – for the next 30 to 250 years. Cold temperatures will reduce the growing season and possibly eliminate some farm lands from production. This will further increase food prices.

Because the future holds so many unknowns we cannot gamble with the world's food supply when the USA has become the Saudi Arabia of natural gas. We can convert natural gas to methanol. The USA is rich in coal that can also be converted to methanol. Wood byproducts can also be converted to methanol. Methanol can replace ethanol in gasoline without any effect on the food supply. Even the Green group Environmental Defense (ED) has voiced opposition to RFS and ethanol in general. We must also remember natural gas is also used expansively in making fertilizer for growing soybean and corn. Even if natural fertilizers are used, the methane release negates some of the benefits of using ethanol.

Government is like an aircraft carrier, it's slow to change course. Once the political tide is headed in one direction, it rarely reverses course. The only way to change course quickly is with the election of officials that will take a strong stance on such issues. We must also keep in mind the EPA has the same power as Congress – they can pass a law with the stroke of a pen. This is another power that must be reined in.

Below is a summary of the RFS from the EPA website.

Renewable Fuel Standard (RFS)

EPA is responsible for developing and implementing regulations to ensure that transportation fuel sold in the United States contains a minimum volume of renewable fuel. The Renewable Fuel Standard (RFS) program regulations were developed in collaboration with refiners, renewable fuel producers, and many other stakeholders.

The RFS program was created under the Energy Policy Act (EPAct) of 2005, and established the first renewable fuel volume mandate in the United States. As required under

T. L. Crain

EPAct, the original RFS program (RFS1) required 7.5 billion gallons of renewable- fuel to be blended into gasoline by 2012

.

Under the Energy Independence and Security Act (EISA) of 2007, the RFS program was expanded in several key ways:

- EISA expanded the RFS program to include diesel, in addition to gasoline;
- EISA increased the volume of renewable fuel required to be blended into transportation fuel from 9 billion gallons in 2008 to 36 billion gallons by 2022;
- EISA established new categories of renewable fuel, and set separate volume requirements for each one.
- EISA required EPA to apply lifecycle greenhouse gas performance threshold standards to ensure that each category of renewable fuel emits fewer greenhouse gases than the petroleum fuel it replaces.

RFS2 lays the foundation for achieving significant reductions of greenhouse gas emissions from the use of renewable fuels, for reducing imported petroleum, and encouraging the development and expansion of our nation's renewable fuels sector.

For information on 15 % volume of ethanol in gasoline (E15), please visit the E15 web page. For all 40 CFR Part 79 waiver notices including those related to E15, please visit the Fuels and Fuel Additives Registration Notices page.

For information on new fuel pathway determinations under the RFS (i.e. petitions for new fuel types, production processes, or feedstocks), please visit the Guidance on New Fuel Pathway Approval Process page.

Lost in Paradise

Amy Lee, and the goth-metal band is for me, no doubt, the greatest ever to create music. I know most my age would not agree – that's beside the point. I was just listening to the song "Lost in Paradise" and thought this describes how I feel at times about my country.

Not since the so-called Civil War has this country been so deeply divided by political parties and ideologies. Americans fight vehemently in the name of their political parties. Even war is divided by party. Each party believes their war is the only one that's just. American people are too often sold a bill of goods in order to fight their supposed just war. If someone speaks out against war they are called an isolationist or pacifist. We repeatedly elect politicians that play those types of word games.

I awoke today to hear Mayor Bloomberg attacking his white opponent for posing with his black wife, saying he is racist for posing with her in a photograph. This couldn't have ever happened in paradise. There is no doubt we will hear one talking head after another justifying the mayor's comment.

Some days I feel so alone. I see the world through my eyes, listen with my ears, and believe I've awakened in the twilight zone. I remember a time when a politician couldn't get elected if he/she whispered raising taxes. Now we have Americans begging politicians to take their hard earned money. I hear those who justify taking 60% of of a worker's income.

I remember friends protesting in the 60's against big government and war. I see those same people supporting both. I watch those same protesters willingly stand with outstretched arms so federal officials can search their bodies at airports. They now stand idly by as male police officers frisk women.

We watch Americans heap praise on a president that stripped away the middle class so there was only the poor and rich. They watched as he grew government at an unprecedented rate. Today that same president is is revered. It took winning a world war to dig this country out from the ravages of Franklin D. Roosevelt's presidency.

While many Americans are divided by parties, there are the apathetic who spend endless hours watching sports, playing games on Facebook, or just lost in a drug induced stupor. There are the single issue voters who cling to whichever party that will favor their cause.

Where are the Americans that support only liberty, even when that liberty doesn't favor their pet cause? I feel lost in paradise because I seek a government that insures all Americans are treated equally under the law. I want a government that is truly blind and cannot see flesh color, hear accents, and doesn't care with whom they have sex. Why do I feel so alone in paradise with these beliefs?

I'm often bewildered by those who send millions of dollars to Africa to heal the sick, when many are dying in this country who cannot afford proper healthcare. Many times those dollars sent out of the country in the name of charity are used as a tax deduction. Those same people then demand government raise taxes on all Americans to help pay for the sick in this country. When government does provide healthcare assistance they will at the same time deny certain services. They ask the same government that too often doesn't take care of wounded soldiers, to provide healthcare for everyone.

I wake up to find a federal government that calls anyone who supports the Constitution an extremist. We now send children to schools regulated by a federal government where teachers cheer when students with passing test scores approach 50%. I found myself in a country where the federal government can take money from people within a state and can then use that same money to blackmail them into passing certain laws, often in the area of education.

The day could be spent listing the things that make no

sense and should happen only in the twilight zone. Someone please tell me that I have awakened in an alternate universe and am no longer in paradise. Maybe I'm not lost in paradise, maybe it no longer exists in this universe. What if the America I want has never, and will never exist?

T. L. Crain

Freedom Tax

Eliminate the Tax Scam

Each year we watch a parade of politicians promising us everything in order to gain our vote. We know that most of these promises will never be fulfilled. We also know that they will blame those failed promises on the other party. I am here to talk about the promises they do keep.

We have amassed a $17.5 trillion dollar debt. We have some telling us that the debt doesn't matter. I'm told it won't matter until we reach $20 trillion. At the rate of debt growth we can see this happening in at least four years. We have one side telling us that we need to stimulate the economy. We have the other side spending more and wanting to raise taxes on the rich. That same side also tells us that we need to stop subsidizing certain industries, while increasing subsidies for others. For those who are unclear, a subsidy is often no more than a tax exemption on certain aspects of that business. This is done to move the businesses in certain directions.

Now let's talk about the most important aspect of tax exemptions. It has gotten to the point that it requires at least $1 billion to run for president – millions to run for lesser offices. Where do they get this money? Yes, you are right, they get it from special interest. Once in office this special interest expects something in return. It is illegal for an elected official to give favors for donations, but they do. That favor usually comes in the form of a regulation that might harm a competitor, or more likely it comes in the form of a tax exemptions. No matter if you vote democrat or republican you are aware of this.

We ask, if everyone is aware, why do they let it continue? People don't want it to stop because the government bribes them with housing subsidies. Each year the biggest tax deduction for a typical family is the house mortgage. This subsidy isn't just for the people, government isn't that caring. They also subsidize the housing industry just like they do most other industries. What people don't realize, is that deduction is figured into the value of the house. If that deduction was removed the value would soon drop to come in line with the market evaluation.

Those on the left and right fervently fight a flat tax or a national sales tax. I suspect this is because many don't want to give up their home or business subsidy. I won't chide you for accepting exactly what you hate the politicians for giving to mega corporations. What I will do is offer an alternative. I propose that we allow only states to collect taxes. A person or industry would never pay federal taxes again. The state would then become solely responsible for all federal taxes.

As it is today, we – the individual or corporation – sends money directly to the federal government. They then decide what portion will be sent back to the state in the form of grants for roads and schools. The problem lies in the fact that money always comes with strings attached. The federal government has a long history of using that money in blackmail fashion to control everything from illegal drugs, schools, and speed limits.

If all taxes were paid to the state, then the federal government would have to negotiate how much each state sends to them. I would assume there would be a flat base rate to insure the funding of our military and other services, while all other monies would come through negotiation and need.

This would completely eliminate the IRS, and that alone would be a huge savings. Of course some states would have to expand their tax collection agencies. This would be no huge burden because the state would have extra money. Some states might not have to increase the size of their tax collection agency because it would already be sufficient. Some states might choose to have a flat tax that would even reduce the size of those agencies.

Paying taxes to a single entity would greatly reduce cost for individuals and businesses. Those savings would be realized in goods and services we buy. This would also take away power from federally elected officials. It is easy to bribe one congress person to amend a bill with a tax exemption. It would be much harder to bribe legislators in every state. Money is power, and the only way we can possibly take the power out of Washington is to take their money. The federal government would find it far more difficult to strong-arm states for more money as they can so easily do with the individual.

It's time we stop using the same old playbook. We have to start thinking outside the box. We must find solutions that would make those on the right, and those who are moderately left, happy. This is not the perfect plan, but it's at least different and could be a start. If nothing else it would make tax collection more efficient.

AMENDMENT XVI
Passed by Congress July 2, 1909. Ratified February 3, 1913.

Note: *Article I, section 9, of the Constitution was modified by amendment 16. The Congress shall have power to lay and collect taxes on incomes, from whatever source derived, without apportionment among the several States, and without regard to any census or enumeration.*
Article 1 Section 9
No Capitation, or other direct, Tax shall be laid, unless in Proportion to the Census or enumeration herein before directed to be taken.

There is nothing in the Constitution that states the federal government must collect income taxes directly from individuals, only that they can. The 16th Amendment could be a stumbling block to this proposal, but it doesn't have to be.

31st Amendment (Freedom Tax)

This is in continuation of my article *Eliminate the Tax Scam*. The only way to solve the problem of runaway central power is to take the one thing needed to support power, the right to collect taxes from the masses. The central government can force individuals at gun point to pay any amount of taxes they decide appropriate. I believe that gun would have less effect on state government.

I believe this is something people of all political persuasions might like. This doesn't eliminate many things the progressives like. A progressive state would be free to operate the same as always. This also goes for libertarian and conservative leaning states. If this country is to survive as a whole, power must be taken away from the central government.

Some are talking about opening an Article IV Constitutional convention. If states are to take that route, the 16th and 17th Amendments are at the top of the list to be repealed. I'm not sure that enough states would agree with the repeal of those amendments. I do believe that if the 16th is repealed with my 31st Amendment, then more states might be agreeable.

> *Note: Article I, section 9, of the Constitution was modified by amendment 16.*
> *This is to repeal the 16th amendment that reads:*
> *The Congress shall have power to lay and collect taxes on incomes, from whatever source derived, without apportionment among the several States, and without regard to any census or enumeration.*

This amendment also repeals Article 1 Section 9

No Capitation, or other direct, Tax shall be laid, unless in Proportion to the Census or enumeration herein before directed to be taken.

Only states can levy taxes on the people. It will be the responsibility of the state to make payment to the federal government. The federal government cannot collect taxes that exceed 18% of GDP. Taxes may not be collected equally among the states.

In a time of declared war the federal government may levy a sales tax on goods that cannot exceed 18%.

Congress shall have the power to distribute taxes without apportionment to census or enumeration.

Satire

A Boy and the Diner

It was a typical Friday night family outing at a small family owned diner. After placing their food order the parents were talking as eight year old Timmy watched the various activities you typically find in such a setting. Timmy's father, Tim, felt someone tugging at his shirt and looked to find his son looking at him quizzically. Timmy pointed to a girl his age cleaning off a table and asked, "Why is that girl doing that?"

Tim knew some details about the diner and replied, "That's the owner's daughter and she helps out after school." He then turned his attention back to his wife, thinking nothing more about the question.

A moment later he felt the tugging once more and turned to see the same quizzical look on his son's face. Timmy asked, "Does that girl get paid? Is it like a real job?"

Tim knew that his son would never understand child labor laws and decided on the simple answer, "I guess you could call it a job and I think they would pay her something." At that moment Timmy excused himself from the table. Dad assumed it was for a bathroom break.

Ten minutes later his son returned. A moment later the diner owner walked over to the table and asked, "Are you Timmy's parents?"

The couple nodded and the man about Tim's age with a touch of gray in his hair asked, "Could I speak with one or both of you for a moment?"

The couple gave each other the "look," wondering what trouble their son had gotten into. Tim stood from the table, followed the owner, and began to think of different ways to apologize for whatever it was that Timmy had done. He mentally counted the cash in his pocket in case there was physical damage.

Once they were out of Timmy's view the man smiled and said, "I'm Paul Taylor, the owner of the diner. A few minutes ago your son approached me and asked for a job. I was caught a little off guard and wasn't sure how to reply. This was so unusual I couldn't say no, but couldn't legally say yes either."

Tim sighed in relief while beaming with pride for his son. He knew at that moment he and his wife were doing something right. The father said, "Thank you so much for telling me this. I'll do my best to explain to him why he can't work – how it's against the law."

Paul said, "This is your decision in the end, but I am so awed by what your son did I want to give him a job, but I can't legally pay him."

The beaming father said, "If you want to allow him to work a few hours on weekends, I'll be glad to pay him. This could be a wonderful learning experience for Timmy."

From that day on Timmy began working in the diner on Saturdays. He started out sweeping the floor and helping the owner's daughter clear tables. Timmy and the owner's daughter became best friends. By the time they were twelve both were experts on the cash register and knew the menu perfectly. When Timmy was old enough to legally work he was put on the payroll. By then he had become a part of the family, as well as capable of doing any job in the diner.

After graduating high school, Timmy took some business classes at the community college, but had little time to go for a degree. This was because he had two big events approaching. One was his impending wedding with Paul's daughter, Amanda. The other was business related.

After the first year of work Timmy began depositing most of his earnings in a bank account. Today that money would go toward opening a diner with his new wife. They would go on to open a national chain of diners based on the one in which he had worked most of his life.

The Teatarian

This was based on a scenario presented by Glenn Beck that inspired me to write this short story. We know because of labor laws even this scenario is unlikely, while in our past this was a common practice. Imagine if the striking fast food workers saw the world through Timmy's eyes.

Obama Shrugged

"The line seems to be moving a little faster today," Jane said to her friend.

Margo smiled and said, "I think so. We've been here only an hour and we're almost to the door. Doesn't the fresh bread smell so wonderful today?"

She replied, "It smells delicious. I'm glad the government decided the lactose and gluten free bread was suitable for us to eat. That will go well with beans."

After Barack Obama's forth term he was appointed the lifetime position as President of the United States. Obama, had promised to fundamentally change America. He had passed universal health-care and to limit cost he had, along with Congress, taken over the farms so that all people ate equally. All foods found to be unhealthy were banned. The medical board decided which foods were the healthiest and would lower health-care costs.

Once the two women had purchased their bread and other supplies, they headed home. It wasn't long before they were walking into the fifty-story apartment building. They smiled at the armed soldier standing just inside. Margo asked her friend, "Can you believe that people used to live in single family dwellings? That was so wasteful of resources."

"I know," replied Jane with a sigh, "I can't imagine such selfishness. Since the ban on single family homes and the passing of climate legislation, we have diverted disaster."

During Obama's second term congress passed the Fair Housing Act. That law put an annual 90% tax on homes with less than twenty families. That created a boon for apartment style buildings. Each apartment had to be furnished and sized to strict standards so that no family could live better than another. There was a complicated standard based on number of children and their ages as to the size of apartments.

Jane and Margo lived across the hall from each other. Jane opened her door and was greeted by her daughter. "I love you mommy," said the five-year-old girl as the government nanny nodded and left.

Jane called Melissa her miracle child. It had taken two years to get permission from the EPA to have a child. Since humans emit carbon dioxide, the EPA had decided to limit the number of children couples could have. They had finally set a limit of two children per couple, but only after the couple had passed a battery of psychological exams to make sure they would be fitting parents. Thanks to such testing, crime had dropped to near zero, as well as the armed military that patrolled streets in search of potential environmental terrorist.

Melissa ran over to turn on the television as Jane was putting away the groceries. The child flipped though the five channels, MSNBC, PBS1, PBS2, PBS3 and PBS4. The little girl settled down as some cartoon character spelled out environmentally friendly words.

Jane heard the television go silent and then her daughter cried, "Mommyyyyyy, the TV is off again."

The mother looked out the window and saw that clouds had covered the sun and the wind wasn't blowing nearly enough to turn the windmills that dotted the rooftops. When the solar panels and windmills could no longer meet demand, all non essential lights and appliances were turned off as the building switched to community generating facilities that were most often bio-fueled and as a last resort, nuclear.

Later in the day when the sun was shining again, Jane began loading the washing machine with the brown and tan clothing. Designer clothing had been banned after Obama's second term. All clothing was functional with looks an afterthought. All but organic dyes had been banned so that limited the choice of colors. With everyone forced to wear the same clothing; that ended envy over who had the prettiest, or the most expensive dress.

Through stringent laws social justice had been achieved. There was no longer a need for sharing the wealth since government provided everything.

Little Melissa had a stomach pain, but since someone on the phone thinks it's not serious, she is put on a month long waiting list before seeing the doctor. Jane doesn't complain since there is no charge and everyone is treated the same. If the voice on the phone was wrong and little Melissa dies, then she is just another statistic.

Obama Shrugged: The Searches

Jane walked out of the department store and handed the package to Melissa. The young girl eagerly took the package since it held her new sweater. The girl had always wanted a sweater, but since Obama placed tariffs on imported knit products, they were in short supply and rationed. When you did have the opportunity to buy knit products, they were priced out of reach for the average citizen. Melissa pointed at the crowd ahead and asked, "What's those people doing mommy?"

"I'm not sure, honey," replied Jane.

The mother and child closed in on the activity and saw a man with a police officer twisting an arm behind his back. The officer said authoritatively, "You go into the body scanner willingly or I take you into the van and remove your clothes where we check you for weapons."

A moment later the officer shoved the cursing man into a black van. People usually stepped into the scanners without incident, but there were still those unhappy with the law. Just as the crowd cleared and Jane started to walk past the scanning station, a police officer said, "Ma'am, would you please step inside the scanner?"

Jane muttered something to herself, but did as she was told. The officer said as she stood in the machine with arms extended over her head, "Miss, your daughter has been selected for random search."

The distraught mother looked at the officer with cold brown eyes and said pleadingly, "Officer. she is only six and is no threat to anyone. I will take the search in her place."

He shook his head and said as she stepped out of the scanner, "The law is the law. We can't make exceptions for anyone. In order to keep everyone safe we must randomly search everyone."

The frightened Melissa was led into the same van the man had been taken earlier and the door closed behind them. Once inside a female police officer led the young girl behind a curtain and harshly ordered Melissa to remove her clothing.

Melissa had been trained for these searches in school. They often had officers come to the school so children could become accustomed to the searches. The children had been taught in school that they must submit to the searches in an effort to keep everyone safe. They had been taught how the TSA searches in airports had been so successful that government had decided to introduce them to the general public.

For at least a century the police had used profiling to catch criminals. In an effort to eliminate all profiling the government passed a law requiring police to stop every one-hundredth person on the street and pass them through the scanner in hopes of detecting weapons or drugs. Every five-hundredth person was required to have the personal body searches. These efforts had been extremely successful – crime dropped immediately by seventy-five percent.

The law also allowed for all businesses to randomly search patrons. This had saved businesses millions each year. Shoplifting and similar crimes had become a thing of the past.

Melissa exited the van and ran to her mother with tears rolling down her cheeks. She said in a low tone to her mother, "Mommy, that woman touched me funny. They told us to report when that happens, but I heard bad things happen to people who do."

Jane's first urge was to charge into the van and attack the officer, but she knew that would only buy her time in jail. She said to her daughter as she held her tight in her arms, "I know dear, maybe someone will notice and fire that woman," but she knew that wouldn't happen. The police were unionized and almost none were ever fired or removed from duty.

Others had reported inappropriate behavior by police officers and had been given a sympathetic ear, but told they were aware these things sometimes happened. But was worth it to keep crime low and people safe. They were reminded the searches were done for their own safety.

Ideological ladder

There are many different ways people view ideological positions. People usually identify with a political party, but when you begin talking with them they have beliefs that cover the political spectrum I came up with a diagram to at least show how I see political positions.

Let's take Republican as an example. In the founding years of the United States they were much like the Liberals of that time. Today it has been filled with social conservatives. In this diagram the Republican Party will be where it should be in a perfect world.

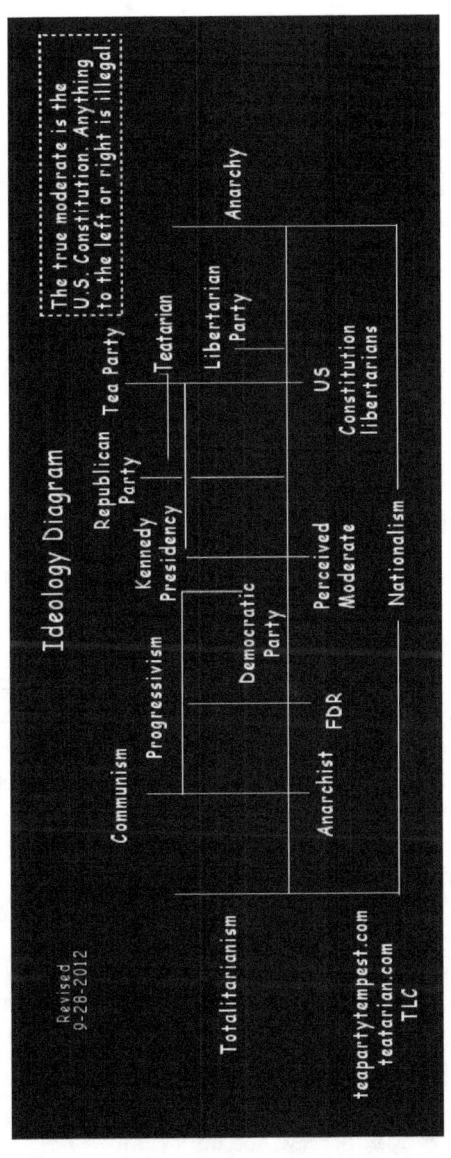

Hobby Lobby Insanity

I couldn't allow the final release of this book without at least a comment on the Supreme Court, Hobby Lobby, decision. This allowed the company to not provide insurance coverage for certain contraceptives.

I often speak of the *Dog and Pony Show* (DAPS) and the *UFO Syndrome*. The left's outrage at this decision is a good example. There have been people standing before microphones, including the president's press secretary, who are saying this allowed Hobby Lobby to continue the practice of not providing coverage for birth control.

This is an outright lie. Hobby Lobby had always, even before the ACA, provided 16 of the 20 types of birth control. Once these lies are repeated constantly on television, many will believe and there is no changing their minds. This has simply become part of the political scam known as the war on women.

I find it even more disturbing that the ruling by SCOTUS was a close 5-4 decision. This means there were 4 justices who would have forced the company to go against their religious beliefs concerning abortions. Hobby Lobby executives had concerns the 4 excluded forms of birth control could, or do, cause abortions. When an individual or group of people decide to incorporate their business, they shouldn't have to give up individual liberties or religious beliefs.

The SCOTUS decision was ironically based on the 1993 *Religious Freedom Restoration Act*. This law was introduced by a democrat and signed into law by Bill Clinton. This law was to allow native Americans the right to legally use peyote in their tribal rituals.

Although SCOTUS struck down the law in 1997, at least on the state level, it is often used in federal cases. If for no other reason to mention this law, it's important to note that in 1993 democrats were fully behind religious rights.

Insurance policies often exclude coverage. Even the Affordable Care Act doesn't require coverage for eye exams and other vision services. Where are protests and lawsuits for this? There are none because this coverage isn't connected to political advancement – the fictitious war on women.

Today is no different from the past. If you don't like the insurance coverage of your employer, you simply find another job or buy the coverage yourself. In this case Hobby Lobby employees could simply not participate in company insurance and enter one of the insurance exchanges.

A good final word for this book is to remind ourselves that we have a duty as Americans to research the facts and to not perpetrate rumors and lies that advance our ideology of choice. The truth should be our best friend and ally when it comes to life.

ACKNOWLEDGMENTS

I'd like to thank all the selfish politicians who made this writing necessary. If not for your desire for personal gain and the need for power, I might have spent this time and effort working on novels. I must especially thank the lawyers in Congress who write vague laws that can later be manipulated in courts.
I thank the readers who suffered through my southern grammar and might have for a second thought about the country in a new light.

ABOUT THE AUTHOR

T.L. Crain was born and raised in Chester, S.C. Trying to understand how things work is a passion for T.L. That passion feeds the creative side. T.L. also writes fantasy novels.

www.ingramcontent.com/pod-product-compliance
Lightning Source LLC
Chambersburg PA
CBHW060244290526
45789CB00001B/187